Designed and edited by Lapis
Via Francesco Ferrara 50, 00191 Roma
tel: +39.06.3295935
fax: +39.06.36307062
www.edizionilapis.it
e-mail: lapis@edizionilapis.it

Translated by David Smith

ISBN 88-87546-49-5

Printed in April 2002
By Palombi Editori
Via Germanico 107, 00192 Roma

ANNA PARISI - ELISABETTA PARISI - ROSARIA PUNZI

ANCIENT ROME
FOR KIDS

ILLUSTRATED BY
LORENZO TERRANERA

CONTENTS

EQUIPMENT FOR TOURISTS

Rucksack containing:
- snack
- drinking cup
- light waterproof
  (in winter)
- sun hat (in summer)
- notepad pen
- camera with film
- this guide book

HOW TO READ
THE GUIDE BOOK

CHRONOLOGICAL TABLE

100 BC

On pages 10 and 11, there are two tables to help you find your way through the different historical periods. The colour scale shows the earliest periods in purple and goes through the various colours until it gets to the most recent ones in red. You won't find the exact dates but you will have an idea of the succession of events and of how long each historical period lasted.

MAPS

At the beginning of each itinerary you will find a map that will help you to find your way along the route. Try to follow it, to know where you are all the time and in which direction you need to go.

THE COLOUR OF THE MONUMENTS

To help you understand the architectural typologies (meaning the types of building you're going to see) we've chosen a different colour for each different type.

⬤ Houses and living quarters	⬤ Baths
⬤ Religious buildings	⬤ Commemorative monuments
⬤ Public and entertainment buildings	⬤ Political, juridical and administrative buildings

SYMBOLS

These symbols mean that the text beside them deals with:

 description of the outside of a building

 the function of the building (what it was for)

 the history of the building

 a story, legend or curiosity

 details to observe or discover

@ means that the subject has already been dealt with more fully on the page indicated by the number that follows this symbol.

The itinerary directions are inside a frame with a coloured background and a symbol like this. Always follow the information looking at the map at the beginning of the itinerary.

A FEW IMPORTANT TIPS

Get together with a friend, the trip will be more memorable and you can compare and discuss what you see.

On your trips around town always try to discover new and interesting things.

Take notes and photos; don't only photograph buildings but your friends too, it will be more fun looking at them later.

The most famous areas are often crowded.
If you don't want to get stuck in long queues try to go when they open or at lunch time.
The best time to visit is between November and February, the "worst" between April and June.

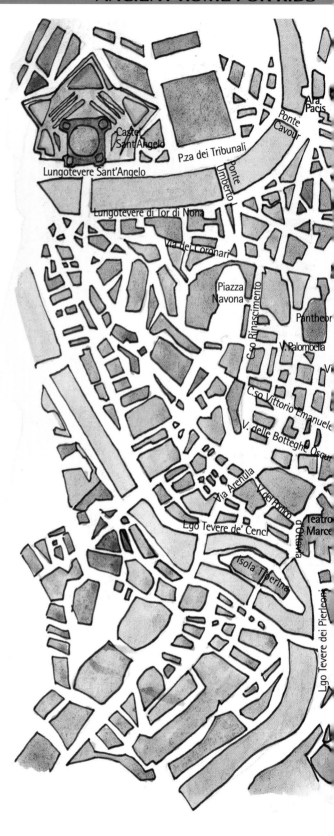

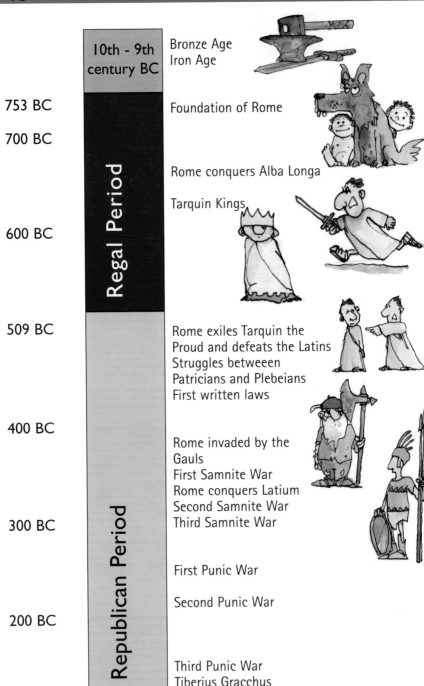

10th - 9th century BC	Bronze Age Iron Age	
753 BC	Foundation of Rome	
700 BC		
	Rome conquers Alba Longa	Regal Period
	Tarquin Kings	
600 BC		
509 BC	Rome exiles Tarquin the Proud and defeats the Latins Struggles betweeen Patricians and Plebeians First written laws	
400 BC	Rome invaded by the Gauls First Samnite War Rome conquers Latium Second Samnite War Third Samnite War	
300 BC		Republican Period
	First Punic War	
	Second Punic War	
200 BC		
100 BC	Third Punic War Tiberius Gracchus Gaius Gracchus Marius Silla Caesar, Pompey and Crassus Octavian, Antony and Lepidus	
27 BC	Octavian defeats Antony	

Date	Emperor	Event
27 BC	Augustus	Octavian Augustus: first Emperor
Anno 0	Tiberius	Birth of Jesus Christ (in Palestine)
	Caligola	
	Claudius	
50 AD	Nero	Rome burns
	Vespasian	
	Titus	
	Domitian	
	Nerva	
100 AD	Trajan	
	Hadrian	Empire at its largest
	Antoninus Pius	
	Marcus Aurelius	
200 AD	Septimius Severus	
	Caracalla	Roman citizenship for all subjects of the Empire
		Widespread persecution of Christians
	Aurelian	
	Diocletian	
300 AD	Maxentius	
	Constantine	Edict of Milan (freedom of worship for Christians) Constantinople becomes capital of the Empire
400 AD		
476 AD	Romulus Augusthulus	Odoacer depones Romulus Augustulus: end of Western Roman Empire

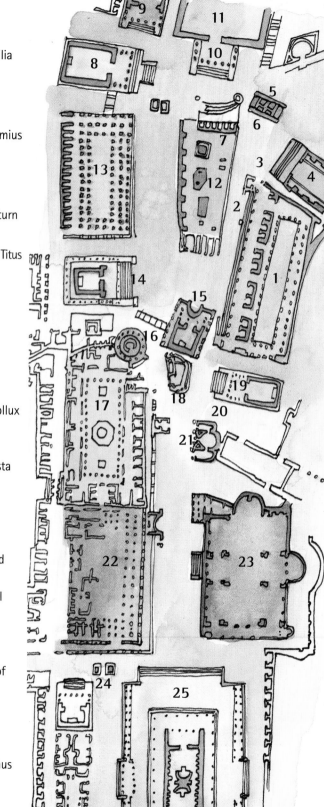

1. Basilica Aemilia
2. Via Sacra
3. Comitium
4. Curia
5. Arch of Septimius Severus
6. Lapis Niger
7. Rostra
8. Temple of Saturn
9. Temple of Vespasian and Titus
10. Temple of Concordia
11. Tabularium
12. Central Area of Forum
13. Basilica Iulia
14. Temple of Castor and Pollux
15. Temple of Divus Iulius
16. Temple of Vesta
17. House of the Vestals
18. Regia
19. Temple of Antoninus and Faustina
20. Ancient Burial Ground
21. Temple of Romulus
22. Eastern part of the Forum
23. Basilica of Maxentius
24. Arch of Titus
25. Temple of Venus and Roma

ROMAN FORUM

Via dei Fori Imperiali
(Largo Romolo e Remo)
Arch of Titus
(Via di San Teodoro).
The Roman Forum and the
Palatine are in the same
archaeological area. Once inside,
you can visit both.

Hours: Weekdays 9 a.m. to
sunset.
Closed 1st May, 25th Dec., 1st
Jan.

The archaeological area of the Forum is in the open air. Go on a fine
day.
Estimated time: 2-3 hours

A very long time ago, in the days when Rome still didn't exist, the few inhabitants of the area were very primitive shepherds who lived in wooden huts on top of the hills by the River Tiber.

They came down into the valley for water or to fish, or to bury their dead away from the inhabited centres.

When Romulus founded the new town he circled the Palatine hill with a wall and a moat so the valley remained excluded: nobody wanted to live in a marshy place full of mosquitoes and difficult to defend.

The Romans frequented the valleys to barter goods and livestock with the inhabitants of the nearby hills, and also to have a chat! Now and again they quarrelled and fought, but with time they learnt to live together and in the end became a united city.

Tradition has it that it was Tarquinius Priscus, the fifth king of Rome, who drained the valley by building a great sewer, the Cloaca Maxima, which collected the stagnant water and ran it into the Tiber.

The valley was called Forum (because it was an open place outside the inhabited areas) and with time it became the main square of the city.

When they had got rid of the last king the Romans proclaimed the republic and continued to conquer nearby populations. The Forum remained the political and administrative centre of Rome. Numerous public buildings rose up around the square and some families built their homes nearby.

Rome gradually became the capital of an immense empire and the Forum reached its greatest splendour. It was enriched with grandiose and highly elegant buildings: people strolling in the square could see how powerful Rome had become and how rich its emperors were.

And what a lot of people there were! Rome had more than a million inhabitants and many foreigners visited the city.

But when the Roman empire's power began to decline the Forum was used increasingly less.

Its buildings, abandoned, were pillaged in order to use the materials for other buildings.

Earth was laid over the ruins and the meadow created.

The centre of what for centuries had been the most powerful city in the world became pastureland for cows. In fact the Romans called it "The Cow Field".

Two hundred years ago archaeologists (people who study ancient civilisations) began to bring to light what was still left of the Forum. That's what you can see today!

Now go into the Forum and try to imagine how it was: splendid, majestic and very crowded!
Politicians came here to take part in the assemblies, to hold meetings or simply to be seen.

The magistrates came to administer justice and city services, merchants carried on business, priests carried out religious ceremonies, the women did their shopping at the market and the layabouts couldn't have found a better place to pass their time.

Also, there was no television, radio or newspapers, so if you wanted to keep up to date on city life and gossip, on the laws that were issued, on how the trials were going and the outcome of the latest battles you had to come here to the Forum, stroll around and listen and talk to everybody.

BASILICA EMILIA

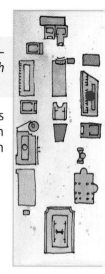

When you enter the Roman Forum the first building you see on the right as you go down the path is the Basilica Aemilia.

It was founded by Aemilius Lepidus and Fulvius Nobilior in 179 BC. It was built on the site of an older basilica and its last rebuilding took place in the period of Augustus.

The Romans built basilicas in order to have covered places where they could meet, administer their affairs and carry out trials on rainy days when they couldn't stay outdoors in the main square of the Forum.

As you can see, this basilica is as big as a square! On the ground you can see the columns that supported the ceiling, and on the left wall the little remaining of the marble slabs that covered all the walls.

Look at the remains of the columns.
How many naves made up the inside of the Basilica?

At the opposite side, in a corner under the trees, look for the copies of some reliefs and find a scene from the "Rape of the Sabine Women" (@ 130).

When you get to the street turn right and have a look, around the entrances to the Basilica, at the remains of the tabernae (shops) built under the portico.

These shops were the domain of moneychangers and bankers.

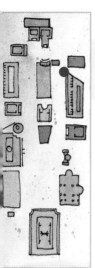

COMITIUM

Go along the side of the Basilica towards the great Arch of Septimius Severus and carry on until you get to an open space in front of the Curia.

This is where the Comitium was, the political and juridical centre of the city until the times of Caesar (first Julius Caesar and later Augustus changed the appearance of the square, moving certain buildings and erecting new ones).

This very important place was used for public meetings (Comitium means meeting) where laws were discussed and essential decisions taken for the life of the state and its citizens.

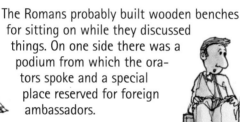

The Romans probably built wooden benches for sitting on while they discussed things. On one side there was a podium from which the orators spoke and a special place reserved for foreign ambassadors.

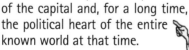

Political decisions had to be taken in agreement with the people (who met at the Comitium) and the Senate (which met in the nearby Curia).

As you will understand, the closeness of the Curia and the Comitium made this place the political centre of the capital and, for a long time, the political heart of the entire known world at that time.

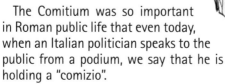

The Comitium was so important in Roman public life that even today, when an Italian politician speaks to the public from a podium, we say that he is holding a "comizio".

CURIA

This great brick building is the Curia, the home of the Senate, begun by Julius Caesar (in 45-44 BC) an completed by Agustus in 29 BC.

Built to replace the Curia Cornelia (which rose on the site of the Curia Hostilia, burnt down in 52 BC) it was often rebuilt. It was transformed into a church in the 7th century AD.

The Senate met in the Curia. 300 senators sat here, and on the base at the bottom the people addressing the assembly took their place in turn.

The Senate was the most powerful political body and only old men with vast experience could be elected senator. The name in fac derives from the latin word meaning elderly.

Go inside and look at the ceiling. You'll notice at once that it's ver high in comparison with the size of the building. This was so as to b able to hear the voices of the people who spoke at the meetings because there weren't any microphones in those days!

In the Curia you can see two reliefs found in the centre of the Forum They depict events that occurred in the Forum during the reign of th emperor Trajan (they're known as Trajan's Pluteuses).

In this drawing look for the objects which certainly did not exist in Ancient Rome

THE ARCH OF SEPTIMIUS SEVERUS

Leaving the Curia on the right, go towards the Arch of Septimius Severus, erected in 203 AD.

The Romans built triumphal arches to celebrate their military victories. This arch was built in honour of Septimius Severus (193-211 AD) and his sons Caracalla and Geta to celebrate the victory over the Parthians and the consequent espansion of the Roman empire.

The reliefs decorating the arch depict scenes from the victorious battles.

When Septimius Severus died, Caracalla killed his brother in order to become emperor and had Geta's name removed from all the monuments so that the people would forget him.
This is why we see cancella-

tions today on the arch where Geta's name appeared.
It is in fact true that Geta did not pass into history but, in compensation for this, Caracalla was always remembered as the cruellest and craziest emperor of the whole Roman period. Maybe only Nero was worse!

Portrait of Caracalla (see the cruel look)

THE VIA SACRA

The road you have taken from the Basilica Aemilia to the Arch of Septimius Severus is the Via Sacra, the main street of the Forum.

Processions of all types took place along the Via Sacra and the Roman population participated with enthusiasm.

The most spectacular procession was the "triumph". A general victorious in war could make an official request to the Senate for one. But such an important acknowledgement was not granted to everyone: the victory was valid only if at least 5000 enemy

soldiers had been killed and new territory conquered! The triumph was a great procession which entered the city and crossed the Forum, following the entire Via Sacra, until it arrived at the Temple of Jupiter on the Capitol where a sacrifice to the gods was celebrated.

The spectacular procession was led by high State functionaries, followed by musicians and people representing the main scenes of the battles won. Afterwards the war booty was presented and everyone could admire the splendid treasures plundered from the enemy: arms, jewels, works of art and even exotic animals. The enchained prisoners were also paraded and at the end, the victorious commander appeared, seated in a gilded carriage drawn by four white horses, to be acclaimed by the crowds that lined the streets to applaud him. The procession was closed by the Roman soldiers who had fought in the war and who, happy with their victory and above all with the payment they would receive,

shouted, sang and made wisecracks. At the end of the parade the leader of the enemy army was publicly put to death. For example, during Julius Caesar's triumph the leader of the Gauls, Vercingetorix, was killed.

Can you put the various scenes of the triumph in order?

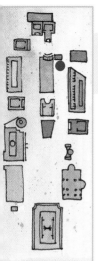

LAPIS NIGER

Right in front of the Arch of Septimius Severus there's a small fenced-off area with marble slabs and a floor in large black stones.

In fact Lapis Niger is Latin for black stone.

When archaeologists excavated this area of the Forum about a hundred years ago they realised, astonished, that the flooring stopped at this point as if due to respect for a sacred place.

In fact, under the black stone there is a small room with an altar and, next to it, a tablet written in a very archaic language damning anyone who should violate the place.

They are the oldest Latin inscriptions ever found (6th century BC) and they speak of a king.

This is why it is thought that a small, very ancient sanctuary once stood here, dedicated to Romulus, the founder of the city, and worshipped at as if it were his tomb. And this is why the Romans continued to respect this area, leaving it intact even when the pavement of the piazza was redone.

Today you can see the stairs going down to the little sanctuary but you can't go in.

There is a fear that this sacred place, one of the oldest in Rome, might be damaged by tourists.

ROSTRA

Now stop in front of the fenced-off area beneath the Capitol.

The first thing you see is a great tribune, or rostrum, with a parapet with many holes.

When Julius Caesar had this new tribune built, the people's assemblies were already being held in the large square behind you and no longer in the Comitium you saw earlier.

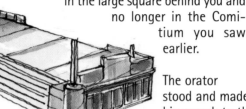

The orator stood and made his speech to the listening crowd below.

There were two small but significant monuments flanking the orator: on one side the *Milarium Aureum* and on the other the *Umbilicus Urbi*. The latter, as the name suggests, was the navel of the city.

The other monument, the *Milarium Aureum*, was a column bearing the distances from Rome to the other important cities of the period.
The Romans measured distance in miles and these distances, obviously, were measured from the navel of the city, that is to say from what they considered the centre of the world!

The name *Rostra* derives from the fact that the tribune was embellished with the metal bow-rams (*rostra* in Latin) captured from enemy ships taken in battle.

TEMPLE OF SATURN

Behind the *Rostra* you can see the remains of some temples. The eight grey granite columns on the left belong to the Temple of Saturn.
It appears that building was begun during the period of the kings, but its inauguration was definitely later, perhaps in 498 BC. It was completely rebuilt in 42 BC and then restored after the fire of 283 AD. This temple is of special importance because the Romans kept the state treasure here.

Every 17th December the *Saturnalia* was celebrated, one of

the most important Roman religious festivals. The most fun aspect of this festival was that for three days the social classes changed places and servants could give orders to their masters and be served by them. But they had to be careful not to go too far! When the *Saturnalia* was over the masters could easily get their own back.

TEMPLE OF VESPASIAN AND TITUS

Nearby you can see three columns of another temple: the temple dedicated to Vespasian and his son Titus; it was built at the end of 1st century AD.

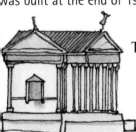

TEMPLE OF CONCORDIA

Another temple (only the base remains) stood on the right: the Temple of Concordia. The foundations were laid in 367 BC. It was built to celebrate the end of the struggles between patricians and plebeians, and in fact the word *concordia* means peace.
Many years later the emperor Tiberius (7-10 AD) decorated the temple with plunder (statues, marble and precious objects) brought to Rome after the victories against the Teutons. After that the Temple of Concordia became a kind of museum.

TABULARIUM

Behind the temples you've just seen there are still many remains of the *Tabularium*, built in Silla's times (80 BC).

If you observe the big building in the background you'll see the different ways in which the upper and lower parts are built.

The *Tabularium* (the lower and older part of the monument) was the state archives, the place where public documents were kept. The upper part is now the main offices of the Commune of Rome Administration and the entrance overlooks the Capitol.

Which one of these kids does not go into the *Tabularium* with the teacher (and therefore does not appear in both drawings)?

CENTRAL AREA OF THE FORUM

Now, turn your back on the temples, the Rostra and the *Tabularium* and take a look at the beautiful square stretching out in front of you. This was the real meeting and gathering point for citizens of Rome: the great area of the Forum.

Now it's closed but in ancient Rome it was very crowded indeed: as well as the people involved in political, administrative and business activities and the layabouts hanging around, you could often find orators declaiming pieces of literature or poetry for whoever wanted to listen.

All in all, the Forum was the ideal place to spend a pleasant day!

This was a really beautiful square, adorned with honorary columns along the right side (there are still several bases from these columns) and surrounded by splendid buildings. Within the square there were a number of small monuments very important in the history of Rome.

First of all you see a flower bed with a fig tree, an olive tree and a vine, all of which were considered sacred by the Romans. They were planted recently because certain documents and reliefs show that they had been in the Forum square since ancient times.

If you look a little farther ahead you'll see another fenced-off area called *Lacus Curtius.*

Many legends have come down to us about this place. Some say there was an abyss here where Mettius Curtius, leader of the Sabines, fell with his horse during the war between Sabines and Romans; others say the soldier Marcus Curtius threw himself into the abyss, sacrificing himself for his city; and others say the area was sacred because it was struck by a thunderbolt, considered a divine event by the Romans, and fenced off (in 445 BC) by Caius Curtius whose name it bears.

There's an interesting thing farther ahead on the right: a fenced-off area with the entrances to underground tunnels which you can see well.

These tunnels were very likely used for the gladiatorial games which took place in the Forum before amphithe atres were built.

The crowd of spectators lined the square and the gladiators emerged from the tunnels to begin fighting. The tunnel entrances were closed when the events were moved to the amphitheatres and later discovered during archaeological excavations.

BASILICA IULIA

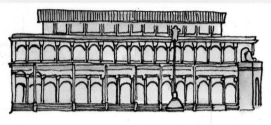

Move on the opposite side of Piazza del Foro and cross a street. This is Via Nova, another important street in the Forum, parallel to Via Sacra.

You can see the rests of a big building: Basilica Iulia, begun by Julius Caesar (probably in 54 BC), completed by Augustus and restored after the fires of 9 BC and 283 AD.

In the republican age there was a smaller basilica in this place (Basilica Sempronia) built in 170 BC by Tiberius Sempronius Gracchus (father of the famous brothers).

The Basilica Iulia is very large, about the size of a football pitch. A great many trials were held in this basilica. When the trial was important the central hall was completely open and the people crowded into the upper galleries as well. When more than one trial was carried out at the same time the hall was divided up with curtains and partitions.

The large number of unoccupied Romans who hung around the Forum also passed their time playing games.

If you search carefully on the steps to Via Nova you'll find the engraved marks that were used for playing a game similar to draughts or morris.

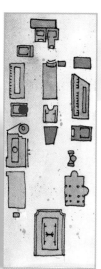

TEMPLE OF CASTOR AND POLLUX

Leave the Basilica Iulia now and go down Via Nova until you come to the remains of a large temple on the right.

You can still see three columns on its high base. This is the Temple of Castor and Pollux, built in very ancient times (484 BC). In the republican age this temple also played an important public role: it was occasionally used by the Senate.

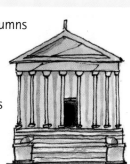

In the course of time this ancient building has been repeatedly restored. The three white marble columns date back to work done in 6 AD during the reign of Tiberius.

This temple is one of the oldest monuments of the Forum.

It was built to thank the Dioscuri or Castor and Pollux

the son of Jupiter who according to legend had led

the Romans in an important victory against Tarquin the

Proud, the last king of Rome SPQR .

This was always important for the because

it proved that also the sons of wanted a republic

in SPQR and not a monarchy.

You can still see how high the podiun of this temple was..
The Romans had decorated it with bow-rams from enemy ships, and politicians often used it when they addressed the people.

(Probably Roman politicians couldn't help organising meetings whenever they set eyes on a podium and bow-rams!)

TEMPLE OF DIVUS IULIUS

The Temple of Divus Iulius, built by Augustus, is on the opposite side of Via Nova to the Temple of Castor and Pollux.

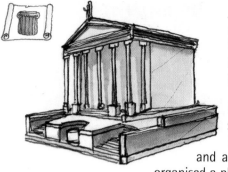

Julius Caesar was one of the most important Roman commanders and politicians.

His growing personal power gained him many enemies and a group of senators organised a plot to kill him.

So it was that on the Ides of March (the 15th) in 44 BC Julius Caesar was betrayed and assassinated while at a meeting of the Senate which, that day, was held in the Theatre of Pompey instead of the Forum. His body was carried to the Forum and burned on a pyre (a pile of wood).

An altar was built on that spot and subsequently the temple containing it.

Julius Caesar's adopted son, Augustus, had his father honoured as if he were a god by dedicating this temple to him; thus also giving great importance to Augustus himself and all his family.

From Augustus onwards it became normal to dedicate temples to emperors deified after death.

TEMPLE OF VESTA

Go back to Via Nova and continue on the right till you come to the remains of a round temple: the Temple of Vesta.

This temple is very old indeed. Its present appearance reflects the last rebuilding after the fire of 191 AD.

Vesta was one of the goddesses dearest to the heart of the Roman people.

She was the goddess who protected the domestic hearth, and that is why it is thought that the round shape of temples dedicated to her derives from the round shape of the ancient Roman huts.

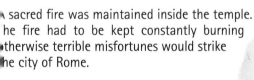

A sacred fire was maintained inside the temple. The fire had to be kept constantly burning otherwise terrible misfortunes would strike the city of Rome.

The only problem was that the constant flames caused a lot of fires which destroyed the temple several times.

During the monarchy the sacred fire was tended by the king's daughters, while from the republican age onwards it was entrusted to the vestals, priestesses of Vesta who lived in the house near the temple.

THE HOUSE OF THE VESTALS

Just behind the Temple of Vesta on the right you'll find the entrance to the House of the Vestals.

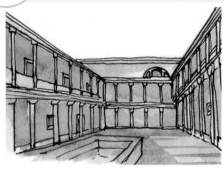

What you see is the result of rebuilding carried out during Trajan's reign and of later restoration under Septimius Severus.

You go in over a little bridge, beneath which you can see the ruins of the older building.

Come to the central courtyard of the house where there are some statues of vestals. At the sides of the courtyard you can see the remains of the small rooms.

The 6 vestals were chosen from the children of patrician families. They remained priestesses for 30 years and during this period could neither marry nor have children. They had to live together in the house which was a sort of convent.

They were highly esteemed and respected, they were rich and could ride through the streets in carriages. They had seats reserved in the amphitheatre. If a man condemned to death was lucky enough to meet a vestal on his way to execution he was pardoned.

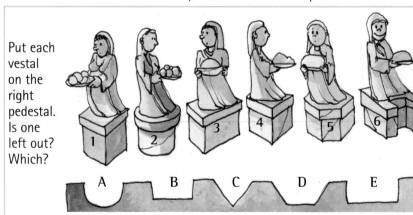

Put each vestal on the right pedestal. Is one left out? Which?

REGIA

If you've followed the route to the end you should be more or less at the entrance to the House of Vestals. Facing yourself, on the right is a fenced area containing the ruins of the ancient Regia.

According to legend it was founded by Numa Pompilio, the successor to Romulus.

Archaeological excavations in the area have confirmed that in the VII century BC there was once a trapezoidal building. It had few rooms and a courtyard with arcade.

The Regia stood for a long time and was rebuilt on several occasions during the course of time.

The original plans believed to be sacred were always respected. The shields and lances belonging to Marte were kept here. It is said that they tremble before every war.

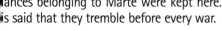

TEMPLE OF ANTONINUS AND FAUSTINA

Now go towards Via Sacra and take a look at the great Temple of Antoninus and Faustina.

This temple was built by the emperor Antoninus when his wife Faustina died, and after his own death the dedication was extended to him. Try to find the dedication in the inscription above.

A church was built inside the temple in the Middle Ages (San Lorenzo in Miranda) but you can still see the original columns in front of the church.

You should note a funny thing: if you came out of the church door you'd have quite a drop and think that it was a nasty trick played by the architect who designed the place!

But actually, when the church was built, the long abandoned Forum was so covered over with earth that the door was level with the ground.

ANCIENT BURIAL-GROUND

Going up Via Sacra, immediately after the Temple of Antoninus and Faustina, there's a fenced-off area.

In 1902 archaeologists discovered part of the great Forum burial-ground here.
The tombs date back to the Iron age. The most ancient being 3000 years old.

The area has been paved except for the ancient tombs which are marked by flower beds.

When the dead were cremated the ashes were placed in a hut-shaped urn which was in turn placed in a round vase. Some of the flower beds you see have the same shape.

The rectangular flower beds contained ordinary coffins of either wood, carved in a tree trunk or "tufo" which is a local stone easy to carve, or terracotta (clay).

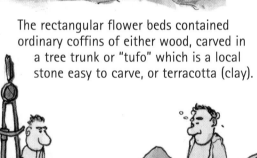

You can see a plastic model which reconstructs the burial grounds and various objects found inside the tombs of the Antiquarium Forense housed in the convent of Santa Maria Nova (@37).

TEMPLE OF ROMULUS

Carry on up Via Sacra and you'll come to the Temple of Romulus on the left.

This temple's name does not refer to the mythical founder of Rome but to emperor Maxentius' son (306-312 AD) who died young. His father is said to have dedicated a temple to him in this place.

Which other temples have you already encountered dedicated, not to a divinity but to a historical person?

But many scholars maintain that this temple was dedicated to Jupiter Stator and the Household Gods.
Together with Vesta, the Household Gods protected home and family.

These gods were worshipped chiefly in private houses.

A chapel or simple altar was dedicated to them where every morning the members of the household brought them offerings (perfumes, garlands of flowers, fruit and other foods).

The bronze door of the temple is the original. It's about 1700 years old and its lock still works!

EASTERN PART OF THE FORUM

Carry on up Via Sacra and you'll come to a me diaeval portico on the left Opposite, take the small street running beneath the trees. You come to a path running along a fenced-off area where there are a lot of monument ruins.

The archaeological excavations still under way have brought to light buildings from various ages.

The oldest structures found belong to the so-named Wall of Romulus.

This is an embankment and moat seeming to date to the age of the legendary founder of Rome (8th century BC).

Some believe it is the wall that enclosed the earliest settlement in Rome.

About two centuries later (late 6th century BC), during the period of the monarchy, noblemen's houses were built over the ancient walls of the now much expanded city.

In the republican period this became a residential area for senators. Houses have in fact been discovered which probably belonged to very famous senators such as Aemilius Scaurus, Cicero and Clodius.

If you look up towards the left you can see the remains protected by modern porch roofs.

Marcus Tullius Cicero

Under Nero's reign, in the imperial period, porticoes took the place of the houses and lastly under Vespasian: the area was used for markets and shops, the remains of which can be clearly seen in the centre of the area.

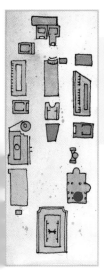

BASILICA OF MAXENTIUS

Go back on the Via Sacra, walk all the way up and at the end turn into the little street on the left. Continue until you enter one of the biggest buildings of imperial Rome: the Basilica of Maxentius, or of Constantine (the former began it in 306 AD and the latter completed it in 312 AD).

This basilica was really huge. You'll realise how big if you look up at the very high vaulted ceilings, 35 metres from the ground, the height of a modern 10 storey building!

There was a statue of Constantine inside which was so big that the head (found in 1487) is taller than a man (2.6 metres). Imagine how much material was needed to build and decorate this grandiose building!

After the fall of the Roman Empire, in the Middle Ages and subsequent epochs, much of this material was removed from the basilicas and used for other buildings.

In particular, in 1613, pope Paul V removed one of the remaining columns and relocated it in the centre of Piazza Santa Maria Maggiore where you can still see it today.

ARCH OF TITUS

Go back to Via Sacra towards the left and go on till you get to the Arch of Titus.

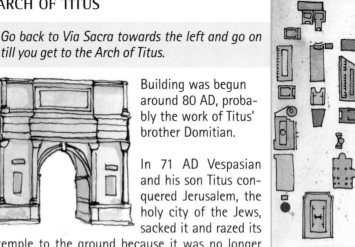

Building was begun around 80 AD, probably the work of Titus' brother Domitian.

In 71 AD Vespasian and his son Titus conquered Jerusalem, the holy city of the Jews, sacked it and razed its temple to the ground because it was no longer recognised. When they returned to Rome they were widely celebrated for this exploit and granted the right to a great triumph. For centuries Jews have remembered the destruction of their temple by avoiding passing beneath the arch, the symbol of this event.

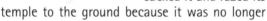

Now go beneath the arch and look at the reliefs on the right and left. Two moments of the triumph are commemorated.

What is the difference between this arch and that of Septimius Severus?

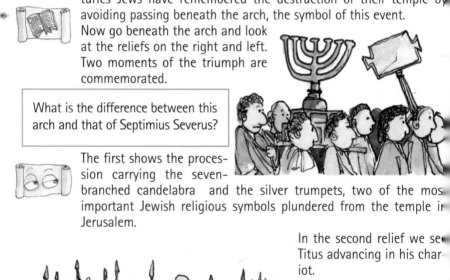

The first shows the procession carrying the seven-branched candelabra and the silver trumpets, two of the most important Jewish religious symbols plundered from the temple in Jerusalem.

In the second relief we see Titus advancing in his chariot.

The goddesses Roma and Victory are together with the emperor. Two characters follow who represent the Senate (a man in a toga) and the Roman people (a person naked to the waist and today headless).

TEMPLE OF VENUS AND ROMA

At the side of the Arch of Titus, between the Basilica of Maxentius and the valley of the Colosseum, there was a great temple dedicated to Venus and Roma, the two goddesses who protected the city.

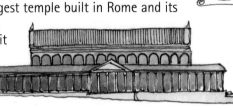

It was inaugurated in 135 AD while Hadrian was emperor and later restored by Maxentius.
This is the biggest temple built in Rome and its architecture is really special: it seems almost like two attached temples facing in opposite directions: one facing the Forum contained the statue of Roma, the other, overlooking the Colosseum, the statue of Venus.

It appears that the emperor Hadrian himself designed this very unusual temple. The most famous architect of the age, Apollodorus of Damascus, dared to criticise the plans and ended up rather badly.
Now the church of Santa Francesca Romana stands in one part of the temple, and there is a museum in the old monastery of the church which contains many items found in the Forum.

Cross the lawn and go to the valley of the Colosseum.

The emperor Nero built his immense palace, the *Domus Aurea*, on the whole area you see here.

The atrium of the Regia was at the point where you are now standing. Here Nero erected his own statue in gilded bronze, 35 metres high (like the entire Basilica of Maxentius!).

When Hadrian built the Temple of Roma and Venus he removed the statue (no longer dedicated to Nero but to the Sun God) and placed it next to the Colosseum, built by the emperors Flavii.
Just think they needed no less than 24 elephants to transport the enormous statue!

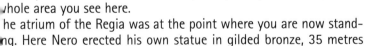

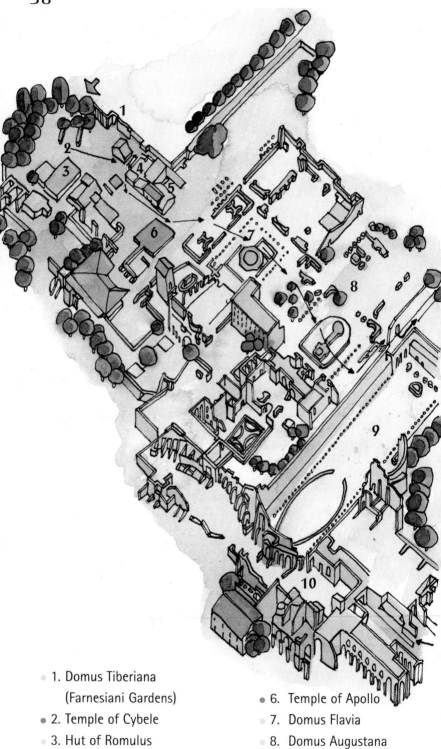

1. Domus Tiberiana
   (Farnesiani Gardens)
2. Temple of Cybele
3. Hut of Romulus
4. House of Livia
5. House of Augustus
6. Temple of Apollo
7. Domus Flavia
8. Domus Augustana
9. Stadium
10. Domus Severiana

PALATINE

Largo Romolo e Remo
Via di San Gregorio, 30
Piazza S. Maria Nova, 53

The Roman Forum and the
Palatine are in the same
archaeological area. Once
inside, you can visit both.

Hours:
Weekdays: 9 a.m. to sunset
Sundays and Holidays:
9.00 a.m. to 1.00 p.m.
Closed 1st May, 25th Dec., 1st Jan.

The archaeological area of the
Palatine is in the open air.
Go when the weather's fine.

Estimated time: 2 hours

Legend has it that Romulus chose the Palatine among the seven hills as a place to found his new city. And in fact remains of a wall and moat have been found in modern times in the Roman Forum beneath the slopes of this hill.

Some scholars believe that these remains could be the "boundaries" of the original Rome. Furthermore, traces of very ancient shepherd huts have been found at the summit of the Palatine Hill.

All this leads us to believe that the legend of the origins of Rome, passed down through more than 20 centuries of history, is not so far from the truth!

For centuries the Romans chose the Palatine for their homes: it was a fine place to live because you were near the Forum but, situated higher up, far from the marshlands, the excessive heat and the noise of crowds and markets.
In the republican period the hill became a residential quarter for rich families.

The emperor Augustus, who was born here, built his new house in the same area because he wanted to live where Romulus had lived. The idea appealed to subsequent emperors who built their magnificent, grandiose residences on the hill which, little by little, became a single enormous palazzo.

In fact the word "palazzo" derives precisely from the name of the Palatine Hill and has survived right down to our own times in many European languages!
English = palace;
French = palais;
German = palast;
Spanish = palacio;
Portuguese = palacio.

ven after the fall of the Western Roman Empire many kings and
mperors went to live, when they came to Rome, in Palatine build-
ngs.

t was only around the year 1000 AD that the hill was abandoned and
ts rich residences became quarries for materials and fell slowly into
uin.

or the next 500 years only a few churches and monasteries
prung up while other areas of the hill were fortified.

n 1550 Cardinal
lessandro Farnese
ought the Palatine
Hill and had a villa
uilt with a marvel-
ous garden full of
rees, flowers and
lants from various
laces.

He thus created the
irst botanical gar-
en in history which
s still partly preserved.

Archaeolo-
gical exca-
vations on
the Palatine
began
about 200
years later.

*To go up the
Palatine Hill
follow the
road that
rises from the Arch of Titus. Take the stairs on your right and you
come to the Orti Farnesiani , the magnificent garden of Alessandro
Farnese's villa which archaeologists decided not to excavate even
though beneath there are the ruins of the emperor Tiberius' imperial
palace, the Domus Tiberiana.*

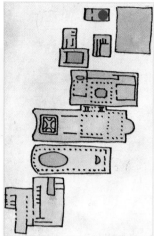

TEMPLE OF CYBELE OR MAGNA MATER

Go right to the bottom of the gardens (with your back to the Forum) and you come to a terrace where a steep staircase goes down. Going down the stairs you come to the area which preserves Rome's most ancient memories.

You are looking at the ruins of a grandiose temple dedicated to Cybele, also known as *Magna Mater* (Great Mother) because she was mother of all the gods. Sit down and read the history of

this ancient temple. During the second Punic War (begun in 218 BC) the Romans were defeated in several battles by their redoubtable enemies th Carthaginians, led by Hannibal. So when the moment for the dec sive encounter came they thought it appropriate to ask help from the gods. Inspired by the Sybilline books (a collection of pro- phecies which we- re consulted in ti- mes of particular difficulty) the Ro- mans sent a lega-

tion to Pessinunte, an out of the way place in Asia Minor, where th cult of Cybele was based. The legation managed to obtain from th

king a mysterious piece of black ston that had arrived from the sky (proba bly a meteorite) and with which th goddess was identified.

They were sure it would help ther against the Carthaginians.

The black stone was carried to Rom by sea.

The Romans won the war and subse quently decided to build a grandios temple on the Palatine for the god dess Cybele.

THE HUT OF ROMULUS

Follow the perimeter of the temple ruins and you'll come to a balustrade.

Down below archaeologists discovered the ruins of huts from a very ancient epoch (9th-7th century BC). You can still clearly see the holes in the ground for the stakes.

One of these huts is definitely more important than the others. So much so that over the centuries it has been restored several times and never covered over by the other buildings that rose up in this area.

This is probably the one the Romans believed to be the Hut of Romulus.

In the same area there is another place linked to the mythical origins of Rome: the so-named "stair of Cacus".

The hero Hercules was grazing his cattle in the area of "The Foro Boario (Cattle Fair)" below. One day while Hercules was sleeping, Cacus, the monstrous giant and son of the god Vulcan, sneaked up and dared to steal no less than eight of his oxen.

To cover his tracks he dragged the oxen by their tails and hid them in a cave.

When Hercules woke up he realised with astonishment that someone had dared to steal some of his cattle.

He began to look for traces but found nothing. At a certain point he heard a loud mooing coming from the cave. Realising what had happened he killed the giant who had challenged him and he recovered his oxen.

AUGUSTUS AND THE BIRTH OF THE EMPIRE

Before we begin our visit to the existing rooms of the house o
Augustus and his wife Livia, maybe we should pause for a minute t
get a bit of background information.

After the Roman State had got rid of the last king, Tarquin the Proud
it was organised as a republic and the important government job
were distributed in such a way that nobody could have all the powe
centred around himself any more. In fact one of the things that th
Roman people feared most was a new king coming to the thron
and, ruling alone, taking away the freedom that the people had won

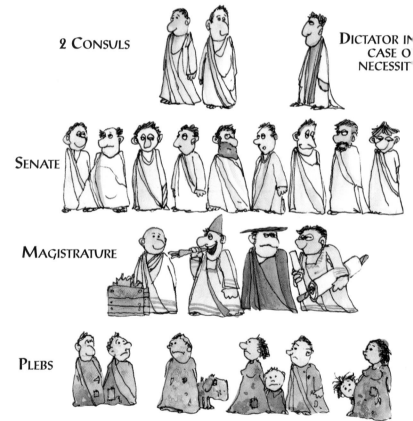

2 Consuls

Dictator in
case o
necessit

Senate

Magistrature

Plebs

Government was administered by two consuls who remained i
power for a year. In cases of necessity (chiefly during the most difficult wars) a dictator was elected with absolute powers, but h
remained in power for only 6 months.

The consuls or the dictator were aided by the Senate and the meetings with regard to legislative power, whereas the organisation of public life (building roads and aqueducts, tax collection, administration of justice, organisation of entertainment and festivals) was handled by the magistrature and religious life handled by the Pontifex Maximus.

In spite of such a sub-divided structure, certain people managed to gain more power than what was permitted by law. Julius Caesar, for example, proclaimed himself dictator for life while at the same time filling the job of Pontifex Maximus. He was killed precisely because he had achieved too much personal power, which was very dangerous for the balance of the State.

Julius Caesar

Augustus was even more ambitious than his adoptive father but he certainly didn't want to come to the same end. So he acted prudently and cunningly. For example, he had his father deified (thus giving more importance to his own family) but at the same time he always tried to conceal the authority he himself had acquired. In fact the Romans realised they had an emperor (far richer and more powerful than the kings of antiquity) when they had already got accustomed to the idea that the State had become an empire and was no longer a republic.

Augustus

When Augustus had consolidated his personal power he moved house and went to the Palatine. It wasn't a random choice to go and live near the place that preserved the most ancient memories of Rome and its founder Romulus.

It didn't matter to Augustus whether his home was sumptuous or very big (he actually rehabilitated some already existing dwellings). The main thing was that the people should link the name of the founder of Rome, Romulus, with the founder of the State: Octavian Augustus.

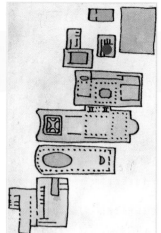

THE HOUSE OF LIVIA

Now go back the way you came, and when you've passed the 7th-6th century BC cisterns turn right and into Livia's house.

The rooms you can visit today were probably the private apartments of Augustus' wife, the empress Livia.
They were part of a larger complex that included her husband's apartments.

 The courtyard and the three spaces overlooking it still have their beautiful wall and floor decorations.
This might give you some idea of the houses rich Romans lived in.

Livia

Of course in Livia's day the colours of the paintings were much clearer and brighter, and the rooms were equipped with comfortable, elegant furniture where the empress could sit and read, lie down to eat her favourite foods, or walk around pondering important matters of State.

THE HOUSE OF AUGUSTUS

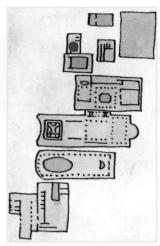

Leave Livia's house, turn back and (after going left) follow a series of republican age areas which were subsequently included in Augustus' property.

The complex containing Augustus' apartments is currently open to visitors each second Saturday of the month.

The house was divided in two parts: a larger, public part where the emperor dealt with affairs of State, and a private part with smaller rooms, all decorated with very beautiful paintings.

Next to his house Augustus had a splendid temple built with porticoes, libraries and rich decorations.

The temple was dedicated to Apollo, much loved by the emperor because it was believed that the god had helped him win the battle of Actium where Augustus routed Antony, the last of his political adversaries.

The emperor also had the Sybilline books moved to the Temple of Apollo from the Temple of Jupiter on the Capitoline.

Placing such an important sacred object in a temple built on his own property contributed to increasing the emperor's power.

Let's hear what the famous Roman historian Svetonius has to say: *"Augustus lived on the Palatine, but always in a modest house that had belonged to Hortensius and was neither exceptionally large nor rich... He slept in the same bedroom summer and winter for more than forty years... When he needed to deal with something secret or didn't want to be disturbed, he used a special room..."*

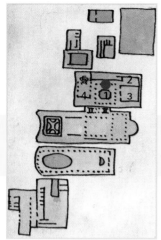

DOMUS FLAVIA

Subsequent emperors abandoned Augustus' sob
life style. From Tiberius onwards, splendid, ev
larger and richer buildings were built on t
Palatine.

Now leave the "Augustan" area of the Palatir
and stroll through the immense ruins of Domtian
imperial palace.

Go into the part called Domus Flavia: this was t
official sector where the emperor carried o
affairs of State,
received coun-
cillors and ambassadors and guided
the destiny of his huge empire.

The central courtyard (1), called
peristylium, can be recognised
from the remains of an octagonal
fountain surrounded by low walls
forming a labyrinth.
Some large buildings overlooked the
courtyard: the Basilica (2), the room where the Council of State m
The emperor took his place at the centre of the apse at the botto
thus also visually representing his near-divine power. The destiny
the empire was decided here, especially in the period after the se
ate had lost much of its power.
The Aula Regia (3) is one of the largest covered spaces ever built
the antique world: more than 30 metres high!
The size of this room leads us to believe that audiences took pla
involving a great number of people. On the other side of the cour

yard there is an immen
room, probably used for ba
quets (4).
From its size there must ha
always been plenty of guest
Their sumptuous dinners we
enlivened by musical ente
tainment and dance and
the sight of a splendid ov
fountain whose remains yo
can see in the nearby room (!

DOMUS AUGUSTANA AND STADIUM

Walking along by the Antiquarium (a modern museum) you come to the Domus Augustana, far more extensive and subdivided than the Domus Flavia.

his was the "private" part of the palazzo, where he emperor actually lived (Augustus was the title reserved to emperors, hence the name given to this part of the building). The imperial palace was on two or three floors with the façade overlooking the Circus Maximus (if you have the chance, look at it from the circus: it's a grandiose sight!) The house was built around a large central courtyard (1) which was on the ground floor.

In the centre of the courtyard there was a sort of artificial pond with a temple in the middle reached by a small bridge. Walking through the ruins of

the imperial palace you come to the stadium (2), a long narrow circus used for horse races. There were porticoes all around on several levels, the tribune for the emperor, dressing rooms and storerooms. The oval enclosure you see on one side of the arena, built in the 6th century AD by Theodoric, king of the Goths, was perhaps used as a riding-ground. Beyond the stadium are the ruins of the Domus *Severiana*, the extension of Septimius Severus' palace. As there was no longer any free space on the hill he had to build a huge, rectangular artificial terrace which you can admire from Via San Gregorio.

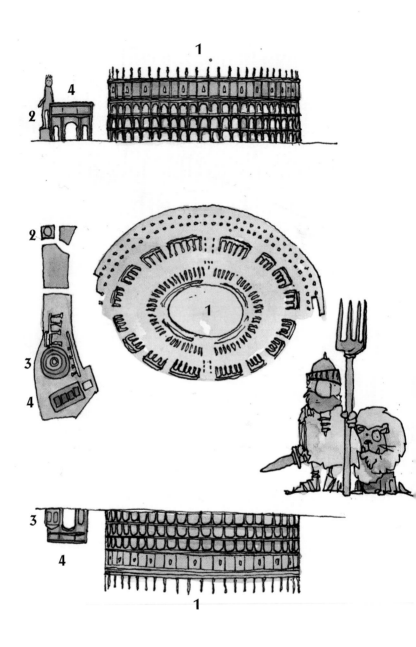

1. Colosseum
2. Colossus of Nero
3. Meta Sudante
4. Arch of Constantine

VALLEY OF THE COLOSSEUM

Piazza del Colosseo
(tel. 06.7004261- 06.4815576).

Hours:
winter: 9.00 a.m. to 3.30 p.m.
summer: 9.00 a.m. to 6.00 p.m.

Closed: 25th Apr, 1st May,
25th Dec, 1st Jan.

The Colosseum area is in
the open air.
Go when the weather's fine.

Estimated time: 1 hour

VALLEY OF THE COLOSSEUM

In the centuries before the founding of Rome this valley looked very different from what you see today: it was narrow, deep and dominated by the surrounding high ground.

The great quantities of water from the hills gathered at the bottom of the valley, forming a marshy pool.

People from the shepherds' villages on the nearby hills came here to celebrate feast days and take part in ceremonies.

It appears that the valley was drained in the republican age, but in spite of this it remained a private residential area.

In the Ith century AD. in this valley new splendid buildings were erected.

The first intervention that profoundly altered the appearance of the valley was Nero's house, the Domus Aurea, built after the fire in 64 AD.

The Domus (which is Latin for house) was in actual fact an imperial palace (it occupied a quarter of the area of Rome then existing) and spread over all the hills you see around the valley.

Where the Colosseum now stands there was an artificial lake where the emperor liked to go hunting.

When Vespasian became emperor he decided to give back to the citizens of Rome all the space that Nero had taken for his personal use.

On the site of the palace lake, work was begun on a grandiose building to be used for shows: the Flavian Amphitheatre, better known today as the Colosseum.

Vespasian also created a monumental fountain, the Meta Sudante, near the amphitheatre.

The area was further embellished with the enormous statue of Nero (by this time dedicated to the Sun god) which Hadrian had removed from the Forum. The Arch of Constantine was the last monument erected in the valley.

THE COLOSSEUM

This immense building, considered the symbol of Rome, is oval-just the right shape for guaranteeing a good view to all the spectators.

The building was built by Vespasian and completed by Titus in 80 AD. The spectacular monument was inaugurated with a ceremony lasting 100 days (more than three months!).

The name Colosseum is certainly not its original name and probably derives from the gigantic statue placed nearby by Hadrian and known as the "colossus" because of its enormous size.

The building (is better seen from the sidetowards via dei Fori) has four rows of arcades, one above the other, in travertine. On each side of the arcade there are semicolumns and above different capitals for each floor. Tuscan on the first, ionic and then corinthian.

The last row at the top, the attic, had 80 squares with 40 square windows. On the inside of this attic were placed large beams of wood which supported the *velarium*, a curtain, perhaps divided into strips, wich protected the public from the sun and rain.

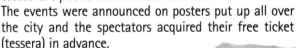

The events were announced on posters put up all over the city and the spectators acquired their free ticket (tessera) in advance.

Politicians and emperors often offered shows in order to influence the people.

Your place inside the amphitheatre depended on your social position.

The emperor and his family occupied the tribune of honour. Nearby there were the Vestals and then the senators who had special reserved seats with their names written on them. The patrician families sat higher up, then knights and, even higher, the plebeians and finally women of plebeian families. There is a complicated series of corridors and rooms inside the Colosseum which were used as storerooms and as cages for the wild beasts. All these corridors were covered by a vast wooden stage on which the events took place.

THE GLADIATORIAL GAMES

Gladiator fights did not come into being with the Colosseum but were of a much older date. At first these events took place on the occasion of funerals of particularly important people.

The great popularity of these fights caused them to lose their funerary character and spread throughout the empire.

Anyone who decided to set out on the dangerous career of gladiator was usually a slave, a prisoner of war or simply a

particularly strong and athletic man who, without a job or a future, hoped to become rich and famous.

The gladiators lived in schools where they learnt the art of combat.

When the moment of the fight arrived the gladiators took up their richly decorated arms and paraded in the arena amidst the shouts and incitements of the crowd.

When they reached the emperor's stage they stopped and shouted all together, "*Ave Caesar morituri te salutant!*" (which means "*Hail emperor, those ready to die salute you!*").

Then the blast of a trumpet announced the duels which continued until one of the combatants was victorious.

The defeated gladiator was not always killed: sometimes he was only immobilised.

At that point, if he had fought especially well, the crowd shouted "*Mitte!*", which means "*Spare him*" otherwise everyone made the "thumbs down" sign and the loser had no hope.

The gladiator's life was therefore very risky, but you must remember that the winner received precious gifts. Moreover, at the end of a particularly glorious career he was allowed to return to a life of freedom.

THE VENATIONES

Side by side with the gladiatorial fights, another typical event in the amphitheatre was the *Venationes*, or the hunting of wild beasts.
The ferocious animals were brought into the arena after having been kept for a long time in the dark without food.
They had to fight among themselves or against hunters.

The scenic aspect of each hunt was carefully stage-managed: hillocks, woodland, meadows, deserts and waterways etc. were constructed to make the shows seem like a real hunt in the open air.

The success of a show of this kind was also linked to the beauty and originality of the stage settings, which appeared in the amphitheatre as if they had leapt out of the earth.
Actually they were hoisted up from the underground corridors with special elevators.
Just think of the extraordinary impression it made when the arena was suddenly filled with plants, hills, back-drops, waterways and hundreds of wild and exotic animals of every kind: lions, tigers, elephants, giraffes, monkeys, hippopotamuses, crocodiles and others that many Roman citizens had never seen in their lives!

Unfortunately, immediately after the highly spectacular part of these games, a real hunt began in which many men and beasts died.
For example Trajan organised spectacles in which 10.000 gladiators fought and the hunt involved 11.000 wild animals!

THE NAUMACHIA

A very unusual type of show took place in the Colosseum (probably only during the first period of its existence): the Naumachia or naval battle.

The arena of the Colosseum was filled with water and hundreds of prisoners of war or condemned criminals had to fight with the typical arms of the armies they represented.

For example, at the inauguration of the Colosseum in 80 AD the emperor Titus organised a naval battle between the soldiers of Corfu and Corinth (two Greek cities).

THE COLOSSUS OF NERO

Look for a high square flower bed in the square: there used to be an enormous gilded bronze statue here, the Colossus. Originally it was a statue of Nero and decorated the atrium of his house (@37). When the tyrant died, his successor Vespasian changed the head of the statue and transformed it into the Sun god. Several years later Hadrian decided to build the grandiose Temple of Venus and Roma in the area formerly occupied by the atrium of Nero's house. In order to carry out this project he moved the statue to the Piazza del Colosseo and placed it on a 15 metres high base. This extraordinary monument was therefore about 50 metres tall, the height of the Colosseum.

META SUDANTE (THE SWEATING META)

Like the Colosseum, this fountain was built by the Flavian family to change the appearance of a part of Nero's imperial palace.

The fountain takes its name from the strange elongated conical shape which reproduces the shape of the Circus metae (meta was a mark in the circus showing the horsemen where they had to turn during a race.) Water gushed out of the top and ran down the sides of the cone, so it looked like a swearing meta! When Benito Mussolini, in the 1933 decided to open Via dei Trionfi, he destroyed all the antique buildings whose ruins were not considered significant. In this way the Sweating Meta and the base of the Colossus were lost. The foundations were brought to light by recent archaeological excavations.

Try to guess:

[1] What were the names of the twins brought up by the she-wolf?
A. Romulus and Remulus
B. Dick and Harry
C. Romulus and Remus

[2] Which of these is the name of a Roman building?
A. Forum of Pasta
B. Hasta La Vista
C. Temple of Vesta

[3] Why is the fountain called the Sweating Meta?
A. It's shaped like a meta and seems to sweat
B. The people sweated a lot while building it
C. It "met a" bad end.

[4] What existed on the site of the Colosseum before it was built?
A. A skating rink
B. A hunting lake
C. A car racetrack

THE ARCH OF CONSTANTINE

The Arch of Constantine is the most important Roman arch that has come down to us. It has three barrelvaults (passages) and is about 25 metres high.

The Senate ordered it to be built in honour of Constantine after the victory over Maxentius on 28 October 312 AD.

The enormous arch, built along the Roman road, trodden by the victorious armies, is entirely covered with decorations that exalt the importance of Constantine as a reformer of the State, but remembering the empire's glorious past.

In this traditional monument, the triumphal arch, were included statues and reliefs taken from the most ancient buildings.

The biggest arch of honour is made up of a puzzle of decorations from different periods.

Why did they choose this type of decoration? Certanly at the beginning of the IV century AD Rome had undergone a period of difficulties and change, when even sculptures and artisans who worked for the noble and powerful moved to the new capital of the Roman empire Constantinople.

But this was not the main reason for using materials and decorations taken from ancient ruins.

Recent studies indicate that the position and subjects used were not by chance: whoever looked at the arch or who were underneath, should be able to visualise the victories and the power of their new master-Rome using well known events that connected the reign of Constantine with that of well loved emperors: Trajan, Hadrian and Marcus Aurelius.

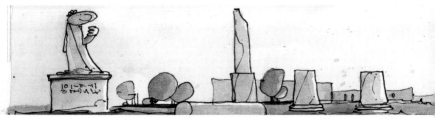

rom that period it became normal to use material from ancient uins to decorate new buildings.

n almost all the new churches built from that period (Constantine ecreed religious freedom to Christians and encouraged the building f some of Rome's most important basilicas) we can find columns, illars, altars and reliefss coming from ancient roman ruins.

ook carefully at the arch:

The four reliefs, two in the centre barrel vault and two in the shorter sides. Should originally have been used to decorate the Basilica Ulpia in the Trajan Forum.

The big statues of Daci warriors above the columns are from the Trajan periods (98-117 AD)

The eight round discs that show scenes of sacrifices and hunting are from the period of Hadrian and ppear to come from an entrance arch of a sanctuary.

The reliefs on the upper part, between the statues, are from the age of Marcus Aurelius (169-180 AD). Show scenes from wars against German tribes.

ook at the statues of the Daci.
1. One was rebuilt in the '700. Which one is it?
2. Do they all have their heads covered with a cap?
3. Do the Daci all have their hands n the same positions?

The other decorations are from the Costantine's period, for example the faces of the emperors have been resculptured with the face of Costantine.

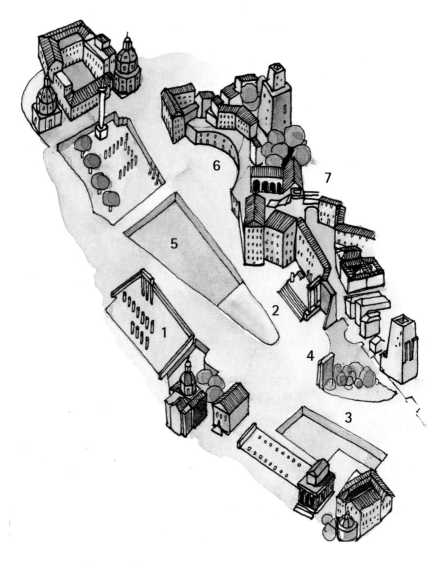

- 1. Forum of Caesar
- 2. Forum of Augustus
- 3. Temple or Forum of Peace
- 4. Forum of Nerva o Transitorium
- 5. Forum of Trajan
- 6. Trajan Markets
- 7. Roman Building in the House of the Knights of Rhodes

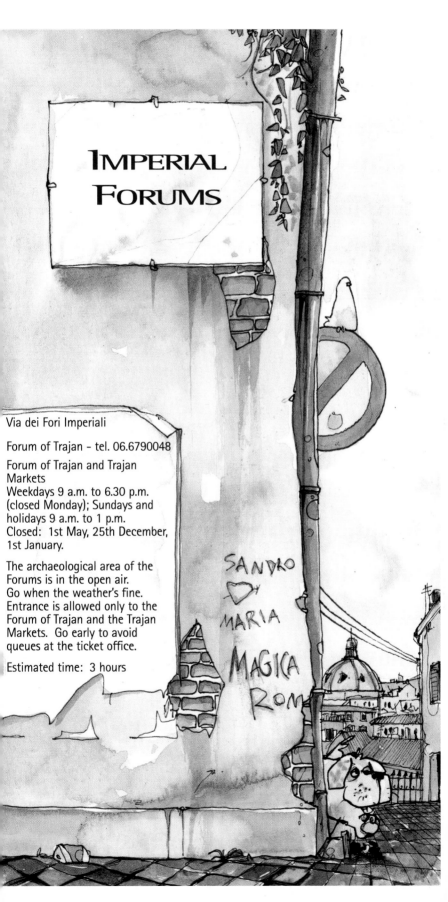

IMPERIAL FORUMS

Via dei Fori Imperiali

Forum of Trajan - tel. 06.6790048

Forum of Trajan and Trajan
Markets
Weekdays 9 a.m. to 6.30 p.m.
(closed Monday); Sundays and
holidays 9 a.m. to 1 p.m.
Closed: 1st May, 25th December,
1st January.

The archaeological area of the
Forums is in the open air.
Go when the weather's fine.
Entrance is allowed only to the
Forum of Trajan and the Trajan
Markets. Go early to avoid
queues at the ticket office.

Estimated time: 3 hours

THE FORUM OF CAESAR

If you want to see the Imperial Forums in chronological order it's best to start from Piazza Venezia, go down Via dei Fori Imperiali (right hand side) in the direction of the Colosseum. After passing the modern statue of Julius Caesar, take Via del Tulliano. On the right are the remains of the Forum of Caesar.

When Julius Caesar decided to extend the old Roman Forum, what he actually had in mind was a far more ambitious project: he wanted his name to be linked forever with the centre of Roman public life. Cicero, a member of the Senate, took charge of buying up an area near the Forum. Its excellent position meant that the price was astronomical: 60 million sesterces!

But thanks to the rich booty he had brought back from Gaul, Caesar could afford it.

Once the land had been bought and the houses that stood on it demolished, building began on the new Forum. It went on for years and Caesar never saw it completed.

In fact it was his adopted son and successor Octavian Augustus who finished it.

The new Forum was a very elongated rectangle surrounded by a colonnade. If you stand in front of the steps, on the left you'll see a series of *tabernae* (shops) of various depths on two floors.

Look carefully and solve this problem:

Number of portico capitals still on the columns	. . . .	−
Number of temple columns remaining	. . . .	+
Number of times Caesar was stabbed	. . . .	=
Answer		

On one of the short sides there is a large temple dedicated to Venus Genetrix, the divinity that protected Caesar's family. In fact tradition has it that the Julian family were direct descendants of Aeneas, son of the goddess Venus.

Caesar's intention in building this new forum was to celebrate not only his importance as a politician but also his "familiarity" and blood relationship with the gods.

For the Romans of the republican age the deification of a man was absolutely unthinkable. But with all his experience of the kingdoms of the East, where

sovereigns were seen as gods on Earth and therefore obeyed and revered, Caesar knew that this was the way towards absolute power. Imagine - while the Romans were building the temple to Venus Genetrix, the Egyptians were building a temple dedicated to Caesar himself, who was therefore considered a god!

The great temple contained a statue of Venus by Arcesilao, a famous artist of the time, and splendid paintings of ancient myths. There was a statue of Caesar and a gilded bronze one of Cleopatra, the Egyptian queen he loved (@ 135). Their love affair started when she, intelligent and very cunning, had herself smuggled into his rooms wrapped up in a carpet. Anything to get to know him!

In the square directly opposite the temple there was a great statue of Caesar on horseback.

THE FORUM OF AUGUSTUS

Go back to Via dei Fori Imperiali and head towards the Colosseum
Cross the road at the traffic lights and go back along the gardens
Find the statue of Augustus (watch you don't mistake it for Nerva's)
go over to it and look down on the Forum of Augustus.

Here we are at the second Imperial Forum, paid for by Augustus from
the spoils of victorious wars. He maintained that the new
Forum was necessary because the two oldest ones
were now too small. But actually, like his adoptive
father, Augustus wanted to create a monument to his own greatness.

The decision to build this square and
the temple to Mars Ultor,
(Mars the Avenger),
was taken (as you may
imagine from the name of
the temple) immediately
before the crucial battle at
Philippi in 42 BC against Brutus and
Cassius, the conspirators who had killed
Caesar. Work on the new Forum went on
for about 40 years.

This square too was built on land pur-
chased from private individuals. It
seems that Augustus wanted it much
bigger but was obliged to limit its size
because certain owners didn't want to
sell him their houses. Augustus was already very powerful, but to
avoid making enemies he didn't
force anybody to sell. The new
Forum stood on an area of
about 125x118 metres and was
enclosed at the far side by a
great 30 metres high wall in
blocks of peperino and Gabine
stone. This was to separate it
from the *Subura*, an ill-famed
overcrowded slum district full
of tenement buildings in poor
condition which often collapsed or caught fire.

The square of the new Forum was rectangular and flanked by arcades with the great temple to Mars the Avenger at the bottom, faced in white marble. In the triangular space of the temple frontal there is a group of marble statues depicting a clearly symbolic scene.

Look at the drawing and find the figures listed below.
They aren't in the right order, and one is missing - which one?
1. Venus, goddess of love, with the child Eros (the Greek word for love)
2. Romulus while tracing the town
3. The goddess Fortuna with the symbols of abundance: cornucopia and rudder
4. Mars, god of war
5. The goddess Roma with lance and shield
6. The River Tiber which the Romans personified as if it were a god
7. Palatine Hill

The Piazza of the Forum of Augustus was flanked by two covered porticoes: the arcades thus formed were decorated with marble or gilded bronze statues of what the Romans called the *summi viri*, the great heroes of Roman legend and history.

Augustus' policy was to leave nothing to chance: visitors looking at the statues in the new Forum must have got the impression that Rome's most ancient and glorious history was linked to the Julian family's, which was Augustus' own family.

In the centre of the square of the Forum there was a grandiose statue of Augustus on a triumphal quadriga.

But what went on in the Forum of Augustus, and who frequented it? The Senate met in the Temple of Mars Ultor when it had to make decisions about war and peace or receive foreign princes who came to Rome to submit to imperial power or to sign alliances.

Here victorious generals laid down their arms and colours. Special ceremonies took place here, sacrifices and solemn public events.

The new Forum of Augustus was inaugurated with the Ludi Martiales (games in honour of Mars) and other games named for Octavian Augustus' illustrious predecessors.

Then a *naumachia* (sea battle) was put on, intended to commemorate the victory of Rome and its Empire over the East.

If you look carefully around the Forum of Augustus you'll find an odd detail: a small staircase hanging from a wall, leading nowhere. It dates not to ancient Rome but to a later period.

Do you know why the small staircase was in this strange position?

THE TEMPLE OR FORUM OF PEACE

Go down Via dei Fori Imperiali to the junction with Via Cavour in the direction of the Torre dei Conti. It's the tallest mediaeval tower in Rome and stands on a part of the Forum of Peace, almost completely buried under the modern streets.

The area which is now occupied by Via dei Fori Imperiali was, until about the year 50 AD, the *macellum*, the Roman food market. In 71 AD the emperor Vespasian decided to build a great monument in its place, commemorating the victories over the Jews.

The monument housed the plunder taken from the Temple in Jerusalem: the silver trumpets and the seven branched candelabrum. It was very much like a forum: a large monumental piazza surrounded by arcades, and an important temple which gave the place its name, the Forum of Peace. Over and above the victory over the Jews the monument was intended to commemorate the end of bloody internal struggles among Romans (69 AD).

Its function was slightly different from the other Forums. It was intended as a green area for the public. Inside there was an actual museum full of works of art. Apart from the works taken from the Temple in Jerusalem there was a series of masterpieces that Nero had appropriated in the East and used to decorate his grandiose private residence, the Domus Aurea.

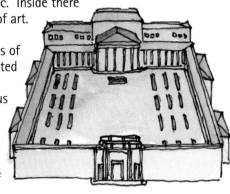

Vespasian returned them to the public, displaying them in the Forum of Peace, a building remembered as one of the most splendid of that period of Roman history.

Unfortunately little of the complex is visible today, but you can see that the Torre dei Conti was built (in the Middle Ages) closely following the square structure of one of the four exedras that stood at the sides of the Forum of Peace.

Now cross the road; next to the Basilica of Maxentius you can still see the remains of the two halls that were on the right side of the temple.

The area which is best conserved is the atrium on the inside of the church of Saints Cosma and Damiano where you can still see the brick walls with traces of the original marble decorations.

It is belived that this space is where government officials conserved property deeds.

One of the most important elements that has come down to us is the great brick wall between the church of Saints Cosma and Damiano and the Basilica of Maxentius.

This is where the Forma Urbis was displayed, a great slab of marble with the map of Rome engraved on it.

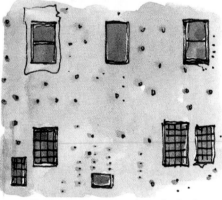

The first Forma Urbis dates to the times of Vespasian but was later redone under Septimius Severus (early 3rd century AD). Fragments of the Septimius Severus version have been recovered; these documents are of fundamental importance, in allowing us to reconstruct ancient Rome and today they are conserved in Palazzo Braschi.

During a recent archaeological excavation fragments were found of what is believed to be the most ancient plan of the city.

THE FORUM OF NERVA OR TRANSITORIO

Go on towards Piazza Venezia, along the Via dei Fori. Past the Roman Forum you will find an area which is cordoned off, the ruins you will see have recently been discovered, they are the Forum of Nerva and buildings from both before and after the Roman Empire.

Certain historical periods have been brought to light, that go from II century BC to 1930, when everything was covered by Via dei Trionfi, today Via dei Fori Imperiali.
In republican times the area was heavily populated, and was called *Argiletum*, which took its name from a nearby cross road.
In this area you could see the rich houses of the aristocracy and the more modest houses belonging to the ordinary people, and areas connected to the nearby *macellum*.
The excavations have brought to light various

underground rooms with mosaics and drains. As the time went by the houses and business areas were substituted with large public offices such as the Forum of Cesar and that of Augustus. The whole area was reconstructed after Nero's fire in 64 AD.
The Forum of Nerva (91-98 AD), was in actual fact, begun and almost completed by his predecessor Domitianus (81-96 AD); it was

Nerva

a long narrow square surrounded by a high wall in Peperino with a row of columns (there was not enough space for a colonnade) end a temple dedicated to Minerva at one end. In the area of the Forum where you are now standing, at the and of the VIII century AD, a large building with an arcade was built (you can see it towards the Roman Forum). It faced a medieval road.

Now cross over the Via dei Fori to see what remains, on the left of the Torre dei Conti, of the decorations on one of the sides of the Forum of Nerva.
You will see the *"Colonnacce"*, two tall white marble columns, decorated behind themm you can see scenes of females working while the upper the attic space, shows the goddess Minerva.

THE FORUM OF TRAJAN

This is the last and most imposing of the Imperial Forums.

Trajan had it built between 107 and 113 AD.

When he decided to build a monumental complex bearing his name, all the land near the Roman Forum had already been built on.

Rather than contenting himself with a space among existing buildings or going to another area Trajan, with his great Syrian architect Apollodorus of Damascus, came up with a grandiose plan, a miracle of engineering that radically altered the appearance of the centre of Rome.

The bold plan involved cutting back the stretch of hill connecting the Quirinal and the Capitol and creating a spectacular monument in the space thus produced.

Having cut through the hill there was a space greater than all the other Forums put together, a space that was also connected to another area of great importance to the ancient Romans: the Campus Martius!

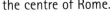

In 112 AD, after 6 years of uninterrupted work, this exceptional piece of architecture was inaugurated, paid for by the spoils of the war against the Dacians, the inhabitants of present day Rumania. It was 300 metres long and 185 wide.
The following year, 113 AD, the Column of Trajan was inaugurated and in 128 AD, 11 years after the Emperor's death, the Temple was dedicated to Trajan deified.

This Forum immediately became one of the city's main attractions and an important administrative centre. Here laws were discussed,

money was distributed to the poor, slaves were freed and teaching was carried on.

Right up to 800 AD the monuments of the Forum of Trajan were still being marvelled at by visitors to Rome.

In 801 AD an earthquake destroyed most of the buildings and only the column remained intact. Then various buildings sprung up in the area, partly re-using the old structures.

In the early 19th century the excavations carried out on behalf of the Napoleonic Government brought to light a great many parts of the Forum.

These works were resumed during the fascist period but completed in rather a hurry. The idea was to form a grandiose background to the newly built Via dei Fori Imperiali with a number of monuments, but this was done to the detriment of the ancient forums which remained buried under the street until our own day.

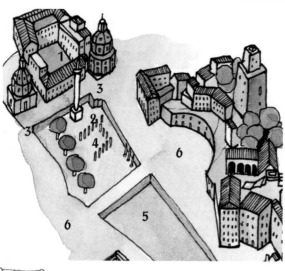

1. Monumental entrance
2. Column of Trajan
3. Libraries
4. Basilica Ulpia
5. Equestrian statue
6. Exedras

Studies and excavations resumed in recent years help us to "see" the Forum of Trajan as it was seen by the ancient Romans who described it as "unique beneath any sky and miraculous ever in the eyes of the gods".

Go into the Forum by the entrance near the Column of Trayan and look at the area from above.

Until recent archaeological finds it was thought that in the area behind the columns, today partially attached to the church of SS. Nome di Maria and Palazzo Valentini, was a temple dedicated to Trajan and his wife. But after excavations of the temple no traces were found!

So to which monument do such colossal

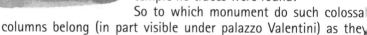

columns belong (in part visible under palazzo Valentini) as they were always believed to be part of the Temple of Trajan?

It would seen probable that perhaps there was a monumental entrance to the Forum for people who were coming from Campus Martius.

After the entrance [1] you passed into a rectangular colonnaded courtyard called the peristilio at the centre of which stood the Column of Trajan [2]. This column is about 40 metres high and corresponds to the height of the earth that Trajan shifted to build his Forum. You can go into the base of the column through a small door. Here, in ancient times, there was a golden urn containing his ashes.

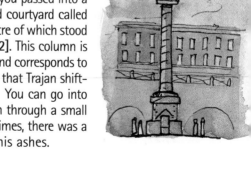

he column is wrapped, so to speak, with a beautiful bas-relief arranged in a spiral band. Books in those days were rolls of parchment (*volumina*). These bas-reliefs were intended to represent a parchment, rolled around the column, telling the story of Trajan's achievements, especially the conquest of Dacia (today Rumania).

If you happen to have binoculars you'll be able to see these scenes. If not, go and look at the details in the Museum of Roman Civilisation.

The statue of rajan which once stood at the top of the olumn was lost in the Middle Ages. The one f St. Peter which you see now was put there in 1587.

t the two sides of the column which, as you have seen, represented n enormous book, there were two **Libraries [3]**, one with Latin and he other with Greek books. These were the two languages known and poken throughout the Roman mpire.

ou can go into the west room f the Libraries which has een preserved under the modern street. The cupboards or the books stood in the iches above the steps.

ake your notebook and try, with your friends, to make up fun story, drawing the various scenes.

ix the sheets together one fter the other so you can roll hem up into a scroll.

Fix two sticks at the ends: this way it will be easier to unroll when you read it. You have made a *volumen*, just like the ones the Romans made.

Continuing, you arrived at the **Basilica Ulpia [4]**. Ulpia was Trajan's family name. The basilica was a large, covered rectangular "hall", the biggest ever built in Rome. Go towards the excavated area decorated with columns, find the entrance, go down and in. This was the basilica, where trials were carried out. Apart from its judiciary and commercial functions the Basilica Ulpia was also used for important ceremonies such as "manumission" by which slaves were freed.

At the side opposite to the Basilica there was a great rectangular square with a gilded bronze **equestrian statue [5]** of emperor Trajan at the centre.

The statue was so majestic that when Constant II, the Roman emperor who lived in Constantinople, came to Rome in 357 AD and saw it he said: "*I too should like such a horse.*"

A Persian prince accompanying him replied, referring to the Forum, "*But for such a horse you would first have to build such a stable!*"

This square was flanked by colonnaded arcades against which two **exedras** (semi-circular structures) **[6]** were located on two floors. The eastern one is still visible close to the Trajan Markets.

The square was originally separated from these by an imposing wall in peperino of which some ruins remain. You can also see the remains of the marble flooring of the exedras.

The rest lies under the present day street.

Is it the temple of Trajan that ancient writings talk of? A definitive answer will be given only once the results of the excavation are completed, but according to a recent theory, we should not imagine it like a classical temple but more as a vast sacred area where the treasures won by Trajan in the Dacians wars were conserved.

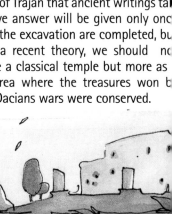

THE TRAJAN MARKETS

With your back to the Column go past the Basilica with its high columns and at the bottom on the left you'll find a small door in an arch. Go through: you're in the Forum of Trajan, opposite the so-named Trajan Markets! Another entrance is in Via Quattro Novembre.

Actually "markets" is a general name to indicate the administrative and business affairs that were conducted in this complex.

A building was created on the slopes of the Quirinal by Apollodorus of Damascus, an elegant structure that had to fit in well with the surrounding architecture.

Looking at the remains you'll realise that they almost seem to follow the cut of the Quirinal hill. In fact their function was also to conceal the cutting back of the hill and at the same time shore it up.

Find the stairs that lead to the markets and go up. The Trajan Markets hosted various kinds of activity.

According to certain scholars there were food stores run by the State, then the market administration offices and also a great number of shops for selling to the public.

At the lowest levels you could buy flowers, fruit and vegetables, while higher up there were oil and wine merchants; at the level of Via Biberatica you could buy pepper and oriental spices, and going higher still there were the imperial storehouses. The fish market was on the sixth and last floor.

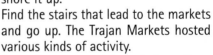

You can have fun going up down and around like in a maze:
try to guess which floor you're on and which shops used to be ther

You can still see a lo
of the old shops,
called tabernae.
They're all built the
same: a square
entrance with jambs
and lintels in traver-
tine.
Above the door,
wooden and probabl
divided into 4 panels

there is a window to light the interior. Goods were stacked behind
the door. Even if fridges didn't exist then, you could still find fres
fish at the market! They were kept alive in tanks with running
salt water, brought from Ostia, while freshwater fish were kept i
water from the Tiber.
There was also dried
salt cod.

Walking around you'll
have noticed an open
paved street. This is Via
Biberatica whose name
probably comes from
the late Latin word
biber, meaning a drink.
The shops here sold all
kinds of drinks. The
street is still well pre-
served and gives us a
unique glimpse of how
the business area of the
day must have been.

Going up you come to the marvellous covered hall where interesting exhibitions are often held.

*When you come out of the great hall of the Trajan Markets you'll fin
yourself in Via Quattro Novembre. Keep going up until you arrive o
Largo Magnanapoli, then turn right into the Salita del Grillo.*

nagine you're living in Roman times.
n the right you would have the impressive Trajan market buildings
nd on the left the Subura, the notorious slum district.

So past the tower on the right, you pass under an arch in the road.
You are now in a small opening: Piazza del Grillo.

 the right hand corner of the square, where the grey stone retain-
g wall ends, there's a building that used to be the headquarters of
e Knights of Malta.

 you get here on Sunday morning around 11 you can go down the
:eps and into the Chapel of John the Baptist.
nis is an old area consisting of a series of pillars and arches.
ok at how they've been built.

ne walls aren't made of normal bricks but of great squared traver-
ne blocks, a way of building that was called *opus quadratum*.

ne place you're now standing in is a four-sided portico which con-
ected the Subura with the Forum of Augustus.

Now turn round in Piazza del Grillo and go on down the street along-
side the big grey stone wall on the right. Behind it are the remains
of the Forum of Augustus. Note the entrances which in ancient times
ed into the Forum (you can still see them clearly today, closed with
jates). If you feel like it, go on to the end of the street. You'll find
hat you're back where you started.

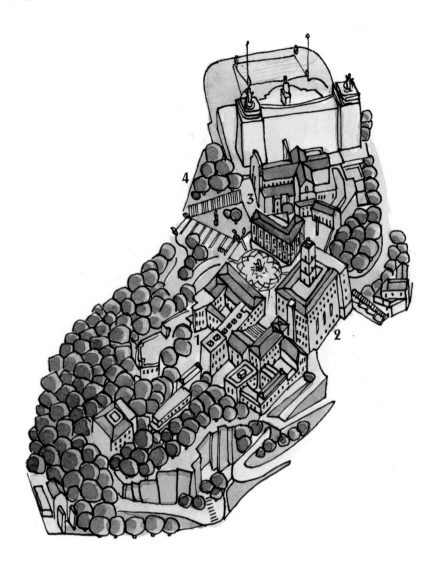

- 1. Temple of Capitoline Jupiter
- 2. Tabularium
- 3. Temple of Juno Moneta
- 4. Insula

FROM THE CAPITOL HILL TO THE CIRCUS MAXIMUS

Via del Teatro Marcello
(Piazza Aracoeli)

A city tour completely in the
open air

Estimated time: 1 hour

The Capitol Hill was the most easily defendable of the seven hills of Rome, surrounded as it was by inaccessible rocks and situated in comfortable position relatively near the river Tiber. The hill had been inhabited since very ancient times (14th-13th century BC).

But it spite of this Romulus did not choose the Capitol Hill to build his house and found the new city.

He chose the Palatine, but the Capitol Hill very soon became an integral part of the city. Tradition has it that Romulus decided to build the *Asylum* on this hill, meaning a place where all men exiled from other tribes in the area could find refuge. The Capitol had a strange shape with two summits separated by a hollow. The first summit was the *Capitolium* (on the right of the present square), the *Asylum* was in the centre and the *Arx* was on the left where the church of Santa Maria in Aracoeli now stands.

The military command was stationed on the Arx because the Capitol Hill was joined on this side to the Quirinal Hill, occupied in the most ancient times by the Romans' enemies the Sabines.

We have to imagine that there must have been frequent skirmishes between the two armies, and for a certain period the hill was under

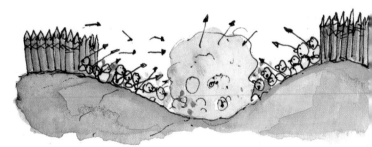

the control of the Sabines. Legend says that the Sabines' conquest of the hill was caused by the treachery of the Roman woman Tarpeia who opened the gates to the enemy.

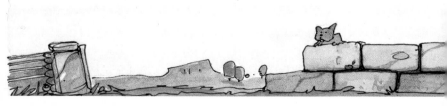

The two hills are now clearly divided (Via dei Fori passes through the middle). They were separated by emperor Trajan in order to build his great forum. He cut through the hill and left his column as witness to the height of the earth he had shift(@70).

But the most important episode in the history of the hill is the building of the great Temple of Jupiter, Juno and Minerva (the Capitoline triad) which since the time of the Etruscan kings had made the Capitol Hill the city's religious centre.

One of the most dramatic moments of the history of republican Rome is also linked to the Capitoline hill: the long siege by Brennus' Gauls which failed thanks to the celebrated Capitoline geese (@132).

In subsequent centuries too this hill remained the religious centre of the great city of Rome.

INSULA

Before going up to the Piazza del Campidoglio, stop at the foot of the steps and look to your left.

You'll see the remains of an *insula*, a multi-storey building divided into lots of flats.

The more well-off families in Rome lived in their *domus*, a detached single-family house, while the less well-off lived in these great blocks of flats, paying rent to the owner.

Usually the ground floor was occupied by shops opening onto the street and the flats were on the floors above.
On the topmost floors the rooms were tiny and uncomfortable, and as there were no lifts they were difficult to get to.
This is why the higher up you lived the less rent you paid.

Side by side with the splendid public buildings and the rich *domus* we shouldn't forget that there were many *insulae* like this in Rome, sometimes accommodating as many as 400 people under the same roof, in shaky multi-storey buildings with tiny rooms, very crowded and with a very high risk of fire and collapse.

CAPITOLINE PIAZZA THE ANCIENT ASYLUM

Go up the great cordonata (a staircase with wide steps so that horses could use it too) which leads to the Piazza del Campidoglio. You are at the centre of city political life (the Administration of the Commune of Rome has its main office at the bottom) and in one of the most beautiful squares in the world.

Its present appearance is the work of Michelangelo (1475-1564), one of the greatest artists of all time.

On the parapet at the top of the steps you can admire the statue of Castor and Pollux, the two mythical twins of Jupiter.

At the sides of Castor and Pollux there are two strange sculpture-reliefs representing the piled up arms of defeated enemies: the so-named trophies of Marius. Nearby there is the statue of Constantine and his son Constant II, then two milestone columns (which measured the distance from Rome) found along the Via Appian.

At the centre of the square there is a copy of an equestrian statue of Marcus Aurelius (the original is now in the Capitoline Museum).

The statue was in bronze covered with gold; in some parts you can still see the guilding.

But according to legend the Romans believed that the statue slowly became gold with the passing of time, a common saying was: "*When Marcus Aurelius's horse becomes all gold, then will come the day of universal justice*".

Marcus Aurelius

Adjacent to the Comune administration buildings you can see a statue of the goddess Roma in a red dress, a statue of the River Nile, recognisable by the sphinx, and one of the River Tiber with the she-wolf and twins nearby.

All this monumental sculpture, as well as the sculpture on the parapet of the stairs, was not here in Roman times but was brought many centuries later to embellish the piazza.

THE TEMPLE OF THE CAPITOLINE JUPITER

In the Nuovo Capitolino Museum (on the right of the square) you can still see the ruins of the grandiose temple of Jupiter, also dedicated to Juno and Minerva.

The temple was begun by King Tarquin Priscus, continued by Tarqui the Proud and inaugurated in the early years of the republic. It wa the city's first important temple and its size wa intended to represent the power of the Roma State.

The building was repeatedly destroyed by fire bu it was always rebuilt, each time using more pre cious materials and more beautiful sculptures t decorate it.

In front of the temple there was a large squareiazza called Area Capitolina where, over the centuries, in-numerable buiding, small monu- ments, columns, statues and trophies were erect-ed, filling every inch of free space. You must remember that for a foreign monarch it was a great honour to bring gifts, including gifts in the form of very valuable statues, to the most important and representative temple of the empire.

TEMPLE OF JUNO MONETA

On the other summit of the hill, the Arx, there was a temple dedi cated to Juno Moneta, dating to 343 BC. You can see what littl remains of it in the garden of the Basilica of Santa Maria in Aracoel

The State mint was here, the place where coins were made. The wor *moneta*, which in Latin means admonisher, came to mean (due to th nearness of the two places) what we today call money, that is, meta coins showing their value and the authority that issues them.

THE THEATRE OF MARCELLUS

Go down from the Piazza del Campidoglio and head left until you get to the Theatre of Marcellus.

In the republican age the Circus Flaminius was here, a building so important that it gave its name to the whole area. The people's assemblies (*concilia plebis*) and games *(ludi plebei)* often took place here and it was crossed by triumphal processions.

In the republican period theatrical performances were held nearby. Though these performances had a great success and were always crowded, in that period there were no permanently built theatres in Rome. Wooden structures were used which were afterwards dismantled or destroyed. The first permanent (brick-built) theatre in Rome was built by Pompey in 55 BC, while the Theatre of Marcellus is the only ancient Roman theatre that has come down to us. It was created by Caesar but completed (13-11 BC) by Augustus who dedicated to the memory of his nephew Marcellus.

The theatre could hold up to 20.000 spectators.

If you look carefully, in the middle of some of the arches you'll see the iron pins that held the enormous theatre masks, fragments of which were found during excavations at the beginning of the 20th century. They can be seen in the Teatro Argentina.

With the decline of Roman power the Theatre of Marcellus was used as a source of building materials. In the Middle Ages floods, fires and earthquakes damaged the ancient structure. The third floor and the rest of the stage collapsed. Towards the end of the 12th century it was converted into a fortress by the powerful Pierleoni family and later, in 1523, became the Buildingof the Savelli family. In 1926 the theatre was restored and excavated to its original ground level.

THE TEMPLES OF APOLLO AND BELLONA

A short distance from the Theatre of Marcellus you'll find two temples.

Of the Temple of Apollo three splendid columns remain, topped by frieze in white marble.

It was first built between 433 and 431 BC.
A terrible plague struck the city in that period, decimating the population of Rome. When the epidemic was over the Romans decided to dedicate a temple to the god Apollo the Healer, believing that he had aided them.
Many years later in 32 BC the consul Gaius Sosius had it completely rebuilt. What you are now looking at belongs to this period.

In front of the columns of the Temple of Apollo you'll find the podium of another building: the remains of the Temple of Bellona.
It was built in 296 BC by Appius Claudius, who built the Appian Way and dedicated to the goddess of war Bellona.

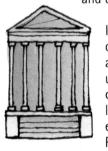

In very ancient times there was a "war column" directly opposite this temple. One of the most important State authorities, a consul or priest, stood at the top of the column when war had to be officially declared on the enemies of Rome.

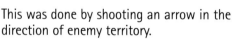

This was done by shooting an arrow in the direction of enemy territory.
The name of the nearby Piazza Campitelli probably comes from *Campus teli*, the field of the arrow.

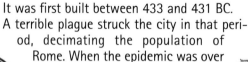

THE PORTICUS OF OCTAVIA

Follow the theatre in the direction of Piazza Venezia. Take Via Montanari immediately on your left and go as far as Piazza Campitelli. Go left into Via della Tribuna di Campitelli. When you get to the junction with Via Sant'Angelo in Pescheria, go down it and you'll come to a part where it widens: you're in the Porticus of Octavia!

The Porticus of Octavia was built by Augustus on the site of an earlier porticoed area of the 2nd century BC. It was a great rectangular area surrounded by a double colonnade and with two temples in the centre dedicated to Jupiter and Juno. Augustus dedicated it to Octavia, the mother of Marcellus (@85).

What you see today is the monumental portico entrance. Beneath the frontal, on the architrave, you can still read an inscription commemorating the restoration of the portico by Septimius Severus and his son Caracalla in 203 AD. Can you find the emperors' names?

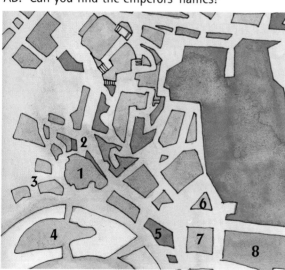

1. Theatre of Marcellus
2. Temples of Apollo and Bellona
3. Porticus of Octavia
4. Isola Tiberina
5. Temples of Hercules Victor and Portunus
6. Velabro
7. The Mouth of Truth
8. Circus Maximus

This is the heart of the Ghetto where in 1555 Pope Paul V wanted to segregate all the Jews in Rome by having a wall built around it. Dominated by the great Synagogue it is an important and characteristic part of Rome and still retains many of the features of an ancient, lower class district.

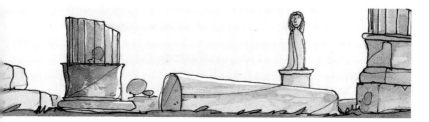

THE TIBER A BUSY THOROUGHFARE

Carry on down Via del Portico di Ottavia till you reach the Tiber.

The Tiber was so important to Rome as to be called "father of the city".

Legend says it was actually the Tiber itself that saved the twins Romulus and Remus by trapping their basket among its rushes.

In the ancient world the simplest way to transport goods was to load them onto a ship and take them by sea using the free power of the wind. Even before the founding of Rome, merchant vessels from far and near (Greece, Spain, Egypt, Africa) had reached the mouth of the Tiber.

As the Tiber was navigable and more convenient than road transport, the goods were taken inland by river.

This required special boats, called *Caudicarie*, which were almost flat-bottomed and were neither sailed nor rowed but pulled up the river by oxen, buffaloes and sometimes men. Just think, this system was used until 1800, the times of your great-great grandfathers, when steam powered tugboats were introduced!

Goods for Rome arrived in this area where the Tiberine Port stood.

ISOLA TIBERINA

If you go nearer you can see the only island on the stretch of the river that crosses the city: the Isola Tiberina. The Romans told many legends about its history.

Many, many years ago (509 BC) the Roman people, tired of King Tarquin the Proud, decided to organise a revolt to get rid of him.
During the great uprising all the grain harvested in the Campus Martius (private property of the Tarquin kings) was thrown into the river, thus creating the island.

Centuries later (293 BC) a terrible plague epidemic struck the city.

It was decided to send ambassadors to far-off Greece, to Epidaurus, where there was the most important temple to Aesculapius, the god of medicine.

The Roman envoys returned by sea, bringing with them the sacred serpent, symbol of Aesculapius.

While they were sailing up the Tiber to Rome the serpent plunged into the water and swam to Isola Tiberina. It was clear to everybody that the god wanted a temple erected to him precisely on that river island.

So it was done. Building was completed in 289 BC and an actual hospital was established in the surrounding area.
In subsequent centuries the island never lost its medical function and a modern hospital stands there today.

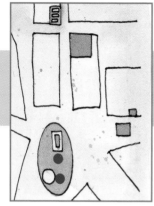

THE TEMPLES OF HERCULES VICTOR AND PORTUNUS

Walk down Lungotevere dei Pierleoni until you come to two temples on the left: one is round and dedicated to Hercules Victor, the other rectangular and dedicated to Portunus.

The Temple of Hercules is the oldest existing Roman temple in marble.

When it was built (at the end of the 2nd century BC) marble was very expensive because it was not yet quarried in Italy and had to be imported from Greece.

A rich oil merchant, Marcus Octavius Erennius, paid all the costs of building this temple and dedicated it to Hercules Victor, protector of oil producers.

The Temple of Portunus is typically Roman with its high base and steps at the front. Portunus was the god who protected ports, and in fact his temple stood next to the port on the Tiber.

Note the differences in the capitals (the upper parts of the columns) of the two temples.

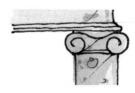
Ionic capital

Corinthian capital

THE VELABRO

Cross the flower bed where the temples are, cross Piazza Bocca della Verità and stop in the wider part of the car park.

This is the Velabro, an area which used to be a marshland full of reeds until the 6th century BC when it was drained by the Etruscan kings.

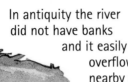

In antiquity the river did not have banks and it easily overflowed, flooding the nearby areas.

Tradition has it that it was precisely these currents that brought the basket with the twins Romulus and Remus, abandoned in the Tiber, to the Velabro plain.

The she-wolf that saved them was said to live in a cave (subsequently called *Lupercale*, derived from the Latin word for wolf) on the slopes of the Palatine directly behind.

No traces have been found of the she-wolf's cave, but its location must have been known at least up to the age of Augustus.

The great monument you see here is the Arch of Janus (which in reality was probably dedicated to the emperor Constantine).

Note its special shape. This kind of arch, which you can go under from all four sides, is called four-faced.

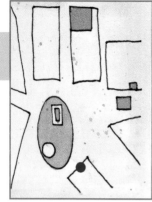

THE MOUTH OF TRUTH

Go into the portico of the church of Santa Maria i[...] Cosmedin which you'll find in the square.

In Roman times there was an important alta[r] where the church now stands, dedicated t[o] Hercules who, according to legend, came here t[o] graze his cows (@43).
Beneath the church portico you'll see a great marble mascaron (grotesque head) representing Oceanus or perhaps Medusa (divinities connected with water).

It is believed that this huge face was a drain outlet of the Cloaca Maxima, the great sewer built by the Tarquin kings to drain this and other marshy zones of the city.

The Cloaca collected the stagnant water and directed it to the Tiber.

The mascaron is called *"Bocca della verità"* (mouth of truth) because, according to a mediaeval legend, anyone putting their hand inside after telling a lie would get bitten[.] Try it yourself, but watch out: it's at your own risk!
And now put your hand inside the Mouth of Truth and answer these questions:

1. Have you ever seen an alien?

2. Do you copy at school?

3. What time do you wake up mum and dad on Sunday mornings?

If your hand's still in one piece CONGRATULATIONS!

THE CIRCUS MAXIMUS

Leave the church portico, turn right and right again into Via dei Cerchi. Go all the way down until you get to the biggest building of all time for games and shows: the Circus Maximus!

Even before the founding of Rome this area was frequented by groups of shepherds.
This is where, according to legend, they held the games in honour of the god Consus which were instituted by Romulus.
The legend says that the Rape of the Sabine Women took place during the inauguration of these games (@ 130).

The circus was built by the Tarquin kings who, having solved the problem of water collecting in the valley, equipped the area with wooden structures and installed seats for the spectators.
In later centuries the great circus was extended, rebuilt in masonry and embellished with statues and small monuments of various kinds.

But let's try to understand how the Circus was and what kind c games went on there.

It was 621 metres long and 118 wide (as big as 6 football pitches i a row!), an elongated rectangle with one of the short sides semicir cular. In the middle, running almost the whole length, was the *spinc* a low wall which at first was in beaten earth but later built i masonry and faced with marble.

Little by little it was enriched with fountains, statues, little temple and two groups of *metae* decorating the end. Augustus for exampl (10 BC) had a grandiose obelisk placed there which had been brough from Egypt, the obelisk of Ramesse II which you can now see in th centre of Piazza del Popolo. Emperor Constant II added anothe obelisk in 357 AD which now stands in Piazza San Giovanni i Laterano.

The Circus could hold 250.000 spectators who crowded on the ter races along the three sides of the building.

On the fourth side (the short straight side) were the *carceres*, the pit where the chariots started from. The terraces for the spectators wer initially wooden, but after numerous fires which completel destroyed them Trajan decided to rebuild them in masonry.

THE CHARIOT RACES

The actual race was preceded by a solemn parade, the *pomp circensis*, and the presentation of all the teams. These were divide into "stables" or factions distinguished by their colours: red (*russc ta*), white (*albata*), light-blue (*veneta*), green (*prasina*), purple (*pur purea*) and gold (*aurata*). Horses, chariots and drivers were a dressed and decorated in their faction's colours, and of course th public also wore the colours of the stable they supported.

But the race is starting! The chariots leave the *carceres* at full speed: the first to do 7 laps wins!
As in any self respecting race, all possible fouls are permitted, such as knocking over competing charioteers or squeezing their chariot against the spina till it shatters.
Each charioteer wore padded leather clothing to soften the blows, but in spite of this protection not everybody was alive at the end of the race!
Every incident was greeted by excited shouting from the crowd.
Usually those who took up the career of charioteer came from poor or foreign families. But if they were successful and lived long enough they could become immensely rich and famous.

Victorious charioteers and horses achieved such great fame that certain emperors (Caligula and Nero for example) did not hesitate to take part in races to demonstrate their ability.

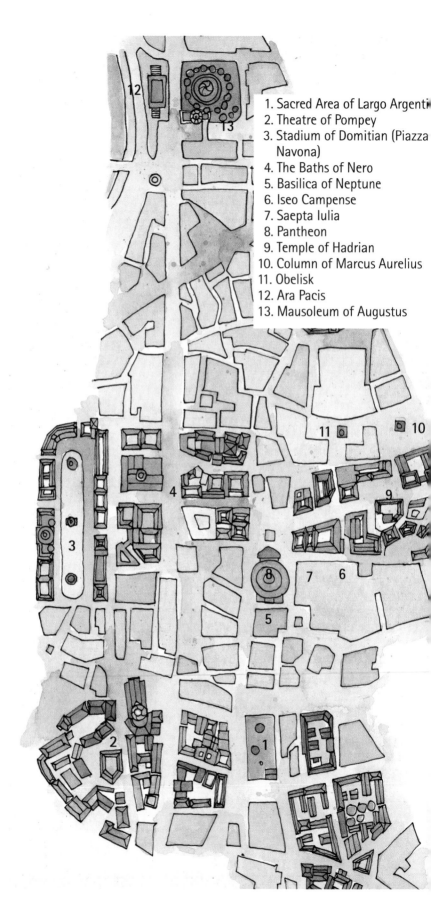

1. Sacred Area of Largo Argenti[na]
2. Theatre of Pompey
3. Stadium of Domitian (Piazza Navona)
4. The Baths of Nero
5. Basilica of Neptune
6. Iseo Campense
7. Saepta Iulia
8. Pantheon
9. Temple of Hadrian
10. Column of Marcus Aurelius
11. Obelisk
12. Ara Pacis
13. Mausoleum of Augustus

CAMPUS MARTIUS

This itinery starts at
Largo Argentina
Pantheon: Piazza della Rotonda
tel. 06.68300230
Hours: 9.00-18.30
Sunday and Holidays 9.00-13.00

Ara Pacis: Largo Augusto Imperatore
tel. 06.68806848
Hours: 9.00-18.00
Sunday and Holidays 9.00-13.00

This route is mostly in the open air

Estimated time for this tour:
2 hours

SANDRO
♡
MARIA
MAGICA
ROM

CAMPUS MARTIUS

The Campus Martius is a great plain between the river Tiber and the Quirinal and Capitol hills. Tradition has it that this area originally belonged to the Etruscan kings, but when the Romans got rid of their last king, Tarquin the Proud, it became the property of all the citizens.

Soldiers were not allowed to enter Rome with weapons. The only people who could

go armed were the police, soldiers of the city garrison and, in the imperial age, the emperor's private guards. So military exercises were held in the Campus Martius, outside the city centre. In fact its name comes from Mars, the god of war.

This great space was also used for public ceremonies, sacred rites, games and various kinds of competitions such as the ancient *triga* (three-horse chariot) race.

In the republican period the Campus Martius became a place for political meetings: here the people elected the city magistrates and every 5 years the census of the population of Rome was taken.

Towards the end of the republican period (2nd century AD) a great number of splendid buildings sprang up in this area: porticoes, theatres, temples and baths. Its face was changed radically. The Campus Martius, flat and without buildings, was just the place where political figures of ancient Rome could erect public buildings in order to gain publicity. This technique was first adopted by Caesar and copied by his successors. These monuments took their name from the person who had them built, for example the Theatre of Pompey and the Temple of Hadrian or, as in the case of Augustus, from the names of his relations: the Porticus of Octavia, the Theatre of Marcellus (@ 85-87).

Even after the fall of the Roman Empire the Campus Martius continued to be inhabited and modified: new buildings, churches and roads have partly obscured the oldest buildings, but some ruins are still visible. You can be an archaeologist and try to discover the ancient city

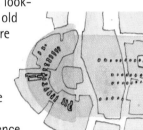

that lies beneath the modern one.
A topographical study, which means a study of the city layout, will help you. Observing the street maps in this area you can work your way back to how it was in ancient times.
Look at this bird's eye view photo of Piazza Navona and observe its strange, very elongated shape.
Fine. Now, looking at the old

map here you'll notice that the modern square perfectly traces the shape of the ancient Stadium of Domitian.
Another example: behind Piazza Argentina there's a small street with something strange about it: in fact Via di Grottapinta forms a semi-circle. Its shape is dictated by the presence of an ancient structure under the modern buildings: the Theatre of Pompey.
But topography isn't the only helpful thing. There's also toponymy, the study of place names: the names of the streets often refer to ancient situations. For example the church of Santa Maria Sopra Minerva (St. Mary Above Minerva) owes its strange name to the fact

that it was built on the site of an ancient temple to the goddess Minerva. Another way to rediscover the traces of old buildings in Rome is to go into the cellars of modern ones: lots of these have been made from the ancient structures.
Now you're ready: start this trip and look for all the possible clues left behind by your ancestors!

SACRED AREA OF LARGO ARGENTINA

This itinerary starts from Piazza Argentina. Go to the mediaeval tower and look over the great space where you can still see the ruins of 4 temples from Republican times.

All the temples in this area face East, where the sun rises. If you've got a compass you can check it out. Scholars have named these buildings A, B, C and D. We're going to describe them in chronological order, not alphabetical.

■ **A**
● **B**
■ **C**
■ **D**
you are here ●

Let's start with **Temple C** (second from the left find it on the map). It's the oldest of the four. It was built at the beginning of the 3rd century BC and is believed to have been dedicated to Feronia,

the goddess who protected woods and vegetable gardens. It's probably the oldest stone temple preserved in Rome.

Now go right, walk along the balustrade to the end and, following the map, find Temple A.

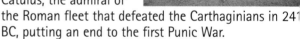

This was built by Quintus Lutatius Catulus, the admiral of the Roman fleet that defeated the Carthaginians in 241 BC, putting an end to the first Punic War.

The temple was dedicated to Iuturna, the goddess of sources and springs. Its present appearance is a result of subsequent rebuilding.
Look for the remains of two small apses with traces of frescoes. They were part of the church of San Nicola de Calcarario which stood on the ancient temple.
The name comes from the work of the "calcararii" who used materials from ancient buildings to produce concrete for new ones.

Go back towards the tower till you come to Temple D.

This was the biggest of the four but is only partly visible because it's hidden by the modern street. It was built at the beginning of the 2nd century BC and dedicated to the Lares Permarini following an important naval victory.

These were gods who protected ships and sailors.

Now go to the right again till you get to Temple B.

It was built in 110 BC, taking up the empty space between the older buildings. This temple is different from the others: circular with two columns at the front.

It was dedicated to the goddess *Fortuna Huiusque diei*, which means Fortune Today, and in fact

commemorated the day of Roman victory over the barbarian Cimbrians, a Germanic people who were halted near present day Vercelli. The man responsible for the deed was the consul Quintus Lutatius Catulus, a descendant of the admiral who defeated the Carthaginians!

There are other ruins in the Largo Argentina area: office buildings, a portico and the remains of a *forica*, a monumental public lavatory.

If you walk around the area fencing, behind the semicircular colonnade of Temple C, you'll see a podium in large tufo blocks. These are the ruins of the **Curia of Pompey**, an exedra where senate meetings were held at the end of the republican age. This place has passed into history because it was here, on 15th March 44 BC, that a group of conspirators assassinated Caesar, right beneath the statue of his rival Pompey.

Following this dramatic event Augustus had the Curia walled up and Pompey's statue moved to another place.

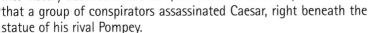

THE PORTICOES AND
THE THEATRE OF POMPEY

In Largo Argentina you saw some of
the most important ruins of republican Rome, including the ruins of the
Curia of Pompey which formed part
of a grandiose complex: the porticoes and the theatre of Pompey.

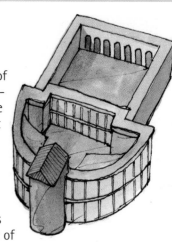

Hardly anything is left of the theatre and its magnificent porticoes
but you can still clearly see traces
of it in the shape and development of
certain modern streets and blocks.

*From Piazza Argentina take Via dei Barbieri (Barber Street) on the
left of the Teatro Argentina, turn left down Via del Monte della Fari-
na (Flour Hill Street) and right into Vicolo dei Chiodaroli (Nailmaker
Lane), then right again into Via dei Chiavari (Locksmith Street).*

These street names are unusual because
they don't commemorate ancient buildings or historical characters but rather
the trades and occupations that were

carried on in this area.
Walking around the centre
of Rome you'll find loads of

examples of this kind. It's fun to
discover that some tradesmen
are still making and selling the
same things that were made
and sold in the same street in
ancient times.
If you look at a street-guide
when you get home (and if you
know some Italian!) you'll find
at least 10 of names of this kind.

STADIUM OF DOMITIAN (PIAZZA NAVONA)

Go down to the bottom of Via dei Chiavari, cross Corso Vittorio Emanuele and pass Piazza Sant'Andrea della Valle and continue straight on down Corso Rinascimento. Turn left into Via dei Canestrari and go to Piazza Navona.

This piazza is another example of "continuity" because it has perfectly kept the shape of the ancient Stadium of Domitian, a very elongated rectangle with one of the short sides rounded. The modern buildings stand on the ancient tiers while the piazza itself corresponds to the former arena.

It was Domitian, the last of the Flavian emperors, who ordered this building around 85 AD. It was intended for athletic games. Because of its shape it was believed for a long time to have been a circus, but more recently it has been discovered that it was a stadium. Horse races were held in the circus while the stadium was for athletics. So there was no central spina, and the obelisk over the fountain was placed here in 1650.

Piazza Navona is and always has been one of the liveliest and most beautiful parts of Rome. Just think: until 1800 they used to organise naumachie here, mock sea battles modelled on the ones the ancient Romans loved so much. For these events the piazza was flooded and the fountain outlets closed, leaving only the perimeter free so that carriages could pass.

If you want to see with your own eyes the way that modern buildings have been superimposed on ancient ones, go to the bottom of the piazza, the curved end. Go down Via Agonale. You'll come immediately to Piazza Tor Sanguigna: beneath the building at number 16 you'll clearly see the remains of the curved side of the stadium.

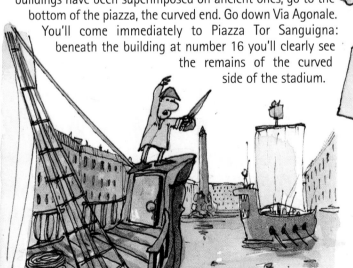

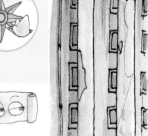

THE BATHS OF NERO

Take Corsia Agonale and when you get to Corso Rinascimento turn right and then left into Via degli Staderari (scales builders). Cross Piazza S. Eustachio and look left.

You'll see two very high monolithic columns (columns built with one single block of stone). These are among the very few remains of the Baths of Nero. The building was so splendid that the poet Martial said: "What worse than Nero? What better than his Baths?"

BASILICA OF NEPTUNE

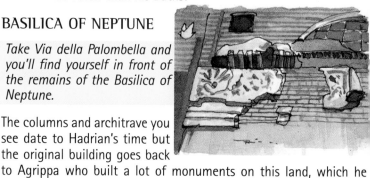

Take Via della Palombella and you'll find yourself in front of the remains of the Basilica of Neptune.

The columns and architrave you see date to Hadrian's time but the original building goes back to Agrippa who built a lot of monuments on this land, which he owned, including the Pantheon which you will be seeing shortly and a great baths complex stretching from here to the modern Piazza Argentina. There was an aqueduct that brought water to the baths and even a small artificial lake! Neptune was the god of the sea and if you look carefully at the marble frieze you'll find some of his symbols: dolphins, tridents and shells!

Reconstruct the sentence. We give you the number of letters in each word, and the drawings will help.

4 – 8 – 11 – 9 – 2 – 3 – 3– 4 – 2 – 3 – 6

Many   to win the   of the

PIAZZA DELLA MINERVA

At the end of Via della Palombella you come to Piazza della Minerva.

This is the church we mentioned earlier: Santa Maria Sopra Minerva, built on an ancient temple dedicated to Minerva. Look at the right side of the church and you'll see the marks showing the levels reached by the overflowing river Tiber!

There's a small obelisk at the centre of the piazza, standing on a little elephant (the work of the sculptor Bernini). The Romans nicknamed it "Minerva's chick" because it's so small.

SAEPTA IULIA

Leave the piazza and take Via della Minerva.

This was one of the most important places in republican Roman life: the *Saepta Iulia*. It was a large rectangular open space (120x300 metres) used for the Romans' electoral assemblies.

In the republican age the people looked forward to elections. There were strict laws aimed at avoiding vote-rigging and corruption. Just think: electoral banquets, processions and demonstrations in favour of the individual candidates were forbidden. On election days there were often violent fights, and at the end of the republican age each candidate had a private army that stood by threateningly during voting.

With the advent of Augustus the piazza lost its original function and became an elegant meeting place for enjoying, or buying and selling, works of art.

THE PANTHEON

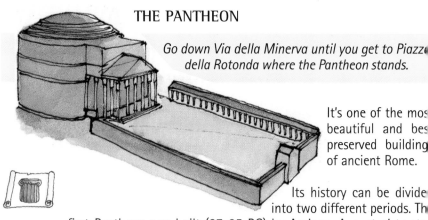

Go down Via della Minerva until you get to Piazza della Rotonda where the Pantheon stands.

It's one of the most beautiful and best preserved buildings of ancient Rome.

Its history can be divided into two different periods. The first Pantheon was built (27-25 BC) by Agrippa, Augustus' trusted friend and later son-in-law. It was very different from what you see today: the front of the temple looked onto the opposite side, and it was built on a rectangular plan as in classical temples.

The second Pantheon was completely rebuilt by the emperor Hadrian who turned it into one of the most extraordinary pieces of architecture of antiquity.

The temple was circular and topped with a great cupola, such a surprising thing that seeing it from outside, surrounded by buildings, it seemed like a normal temple. But nobody expected, on going inside, to find that it was round!

Its perfectly preserved state is due to the fact that in the year 608 AD the Pantheon was presented by the Byzantine emperor Phocas to Pope Boniface IV who had it consecrated as the Church of All Martyrs.

A few years later another Byzantine emperor, Constant II, robbed the monument of the splendid bronze tiles that covered the cupola.

1000 years later another Pope, Urban VIII, whose surname was Barberini, dismantled the bronze beams of the portal to have them melted down and used for the baldachin of St. Peter's. But there was so much bronze that it was also used to make dozens of cannons for Castel Sant' Angelo, the Pope's stronghold.

In Rome they say: "What the barbarians didn't do, the Barberinis did", meaning that what the barbarians spared was destroyed by the Barberini family!

Go in and look around. The building almost seems to enfold you. This impression is due to its very special shape: it's like putting a perfect sphere into a cylinder whose height is the same as the radius of the sphere.

The cupola that tops the building is the biggest ever built in the ancient world. It's made of materials that get increasingly lighter the nearer you get to the top. Volcanic pumice stone was used for the highest part. If you've never seen any, ask someone to give you a piece. You'll be struck by how little it weighs!

The only source of light is the great hole in the centre of the cupola. There must have been statues of the gods in the niches you can see along the walls.
Today there are tombs of famous artists and past kings. How many of them have you heard of?
Have you ever wondered what the name Pantheon means? It's Greek for all gods (*pan* = all, *teos* = god) and in fact the building was dedicated to them.

There's a legend about the place the building stands on. One day Romulus, the mythical founder of Rome, was enveloped by a cloud and disappeared from sight. From that moment Romulus was never seen again and tradition has it that he ascended among the immortal gods. Cultured Romans didn't really believe the story, but the place had become symbolic and this was one of the reasons why Agrippa chose it.

When you leave the Pantheon stop again and look at it from outside. Try to read the great inscription:

M.AGRIPPA L:F: COS TERTIUM FECIT

The phrase means: "it was done by Marcus Agrippa, son of Lucius, when he was Consul for the third time" (L:F: COS = *Luci Filius Consul*). But this refers to the first Pantheon. What's it doing on a monument rebuilt by Hadrian? Emperor Hadrian wanted to leave the name of the founder of the temple, thus linking his new building with the most beloved personality of the first years of the Empire.

TEMPLE OF HADRIAN

Take Via dei Pastini and go all the way down until you get to Piazza di Pietra.

The most prominent ruins of the temple of Hadrian are here. You'll find a large building that combines ancient and modern: it is the headquarters of the Stock Exchange, while the ancient ruins are the remains of the Temple of Hadrian, dedicated to him by his successor Antoninus Pius in 145 AD.

Look carefully at the reconstruction at the side. The colonnade you can still see today was the right side of the building which had no less than 8 columns on the short sides and 15 on the long. It stood on a 4 metre high podium.

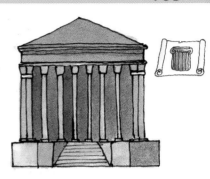

The building, completely faced in splendid marble, was richly decorated inside with reliefs representing the 38 provinces of the Empire which, exactly in those years, had reached its greatest size ever.

If you want you can still see them today, in the courtyard of the Palazzo dei Conservatori in the Capitoline Museums.

Though they depict defeated peoples these reliefs are not images of prisoners bowed down under the weight of Roman power. In fact during Hadrian's reign, which was characterised by peace and good administration, the role of the citizens of the provinces became fundamental to the life of the Roman State and they were no longer considered as mere subjects. The temple was surrounded by a great porticoed piazza, and there were two other important buildings in this same area.

Emperor Hadrian didn't just build a grandiose monument in honour of his mother Marciana but also did the same for his mother-in-law Matidia.

A decidedly unusual thing for a man to do in any period of history. Almost nothing remains of the Temple and Basilica of Matidia or the Temple of Marciana. The Temple of Matidia must have been colossal, perhaps the biggest ever built in Rome, with columns about 17 metres high - as high as a 6 storey building!

THE COLUMN OF MARCUS AURELIUS

Leaving the Temple of Hadrian behind you and taking Via de Bergamaschi on your right you'll soon see the impressive Colum of Marcus Aurelius.

It was built after 180 AD (the year Marcus Aurelius die and was modelled on the famous Column of Trajan. Thi column too tells the story of the emperor's deeds agains the Barbarians.

There is a series of connected episodes unrolled like a *vo. umen*, the ancient Roman scroll.

The column was built with 28 huge hollowed-out drums placed one on top of the other.

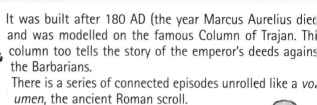

In fact there's a steep spiral staircase inside with 190 steps going up to the terrace where originally there was a statue of Marcus Aurelius.

During restorations in 1589 the statue - lost i the Middle Ages - was replaced by one of S Paul. On the same occasion the reliefs that dec orated the base were destroyed and replaced b an inscription that mistakenly attributed the co umn to the emperor Antoninus Pius!

One side of the Piazza looks onto the modern Vi del Corso. Where the big modern buildings ar today there was a large built-up area with tene ment houses, arcades and shops which stretche to the slopes of the Quirinal.

Take Via della Colonna Antonina and go to Piazza Montecitorio.

Here you will find the great building where th Chamber of Deputies meets. In ancient times i was the place chosen for the ceremony of cre mating the Emperor. The remains of two *ustrin* have been found here, the square enclosure where the ceremonies took place.

OBELISK OF PSAMMETICHUS II: AUGUSTUS' SUNDIAL

In the centre of the square you can see the Obelisk of Psammetichus II. It originally stood in Egypt, in Heliopolis (a Greek word meaning City of the Sun) but Octavian Augustus took it and brought it to Rome to use as a gigantic marker for his sundial.

In ancient times clocks didn't exist but people still had to know how to measure time.

So, long before Roma times, the day was already divided into smaller units (hours) and instruments had been created which told you the exact hour of the day: sun clocks, or sundials.

Augustus' clock was grandiose: it took up an entire square and its dial was inscribed on the ground where the shadow of the obelisk showed the passage of time. The inscription still visible on the base of the obelisk refers to the dedication Augustus made to the Sun.

According to the Latin historian Pliny, the sundial was supposed to receive the shadow of the sun and thus establish the length of day and night".

IMP·CAESAR·DIVI·F.
· AVGVSTVS
PONTIFEX MAXIMVS
IMP·XII COS XI TRIBPOT
AEGVI TO IN POTESTATUM
SOLIDONVM DEDIT

When, as a result of earthquakes and the raising of the ground level, the sundial no longer functioned the emperor Domitian (80 AD) had it restored.

Recent excavations have revealed traces of the paving very near to the area where you are now.

But this sundial wasn't just a useful thing. Some scholars say that on 23rd September, Augustus' birthday, the shadow fell on the Ara Pacis!

When this area was excavated in 1748 the obelisk was re-erected. It was restored with material from another monument rediscovered at the same time: the Column of Antoninus Pius.

It was different from the honorary columns of Trajan and Marcus Aurelius because its high shaft was plain, not decorated.

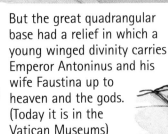

But the great quadrangular base had a relief in which a young winged divinity carries Emperor Antoninus and his wife Faustina up to heaven and the gods. (Today it is in the Vatican Museums)

Observe at the photo:
There are two figures beneath the winged divinity: the goddess Roma on the right and the personification of Campus Martius on the left.

1. What is Campus Martius holding in his hand?
a) a lance
b) an obelisk
c) the hand of a clock

2. What has the goddess Roma got under her left arm?
a) a huge decorated lid
b) a shield
c) a sun hat

3. What birds are flying on each side of the Emperor and his wife?
a) two condors   b) two crows
c) two eagles

THE ARA PACIS

Follow the Chamber of Deputies on the left, taking Via della Missione, and from Piazza del Parlamento take Via di Campo Marzio. Cross Piazza della Torretta, Piazza San Lorenzo in Lucina and continue down Via del Leoncino. In Via Tomacelli turn left and, where it widens, turn right. You'll see the Ara Pacis on the left. Go there.

In 13 BC the senate voted to build the Ara Pacis to celebrate Augustus' return to Rome after his victorious military campaigns in Spain and Gaul, but three years passed before it was completed.

It was inaugurated on 30th January in 9 BC, the birthday of Augustus' wife Livia.

Before going in, look at the base: there is a copy of Augustus' testament, the Res Gestae ("achievements") which lists his achievements in politics, war and economics.

Originally the monument wasn't here. It was discovered in fragments during various excavations in the area of the church of San Lorenzo in Lucina. The last, in 1937-38, brought to light so much material that it was decided to rebuild the monument in a different place. On the sides of the entrance you can see two episodes connected with Rome's most ancient and legendary history.

The relief on the left showed the discovery of Romulus and Remus being suckled by the she-wolf. The god Mars was on the left and the shepherd Faustulus, who found and brought up the mythical twins, was on the right.

The relief on the right of the entrance much better preserved and shows Aenea the founder of the Julian line. He's th bearded one on the right preparing a sacri fice to the Household Gods.

Now go and look at the reliefs on the opposite side of the enclosure. On the left of the door you can see three seated figures. The one in the middle is *Tellus*, the personification of fertile land. And in fact she's portrayed as a beautiful woman with two children sitting on her knees. The children represent the fruits of the earth. There are two nymphs at the sides. The one on the left, seated on a swan, symbolises the elements of the air while the one on the right is on a sea dragon,

personifying the elements of water. For Augustus had in fact inau gurated an age of universa peace on land and at sea.

Now go left to the side of the altar that faces the Mausoleum of Augustus. You'll find a line of people in procession.

Augustus himself **(A)** fol lowed by priests. Agrippa **(B)**, Augustus' friend and son-in-law. Gaiu Caesar **(C)** in typical Greek clothing. Some say that this woman **(D** is Augustus' wife Livia. When they married she already had two chil dren from a previous marriage: Tiberius **(E)** and Drusus **(H)** with hi wife Antonia **(F)** and their son Germanicus **(G)** holding his mother' hand. The others are all members of Augustus' family. On the othe side look for Lucius Caesar, a small child with his arms uplifted wanting to be picked up. With this splendid monument Augustus lef a visible sign of the new age he had brought in. It was an altar ded icated to peace and also a sign ththe new empire was founded on a dynasty.

THE MAUSOLEUM OF AUGUSTUS

Go down the steps now and head left in the direction of the ruins of the great tomb Augustus built for himself and his family.

Having defeated Antony in Egypt, Augustus left Alexandria for Rome. It was 29 BC and his power was by now absolute. So he decided to set about building a grandiose family tomb. The architectural model he chose was perhaps based on the tombs of famous figures of the East such as Alexander the Great.

This was also reflected in the name given to the tomb: mausoleum, like the most famous sovereign's tomb then known, that of King Mausolus of Caria. Its appearance has been radically altered by the ups and downs of 2000 years of history.

It was a great circular building with concentric walls, standing on a roughly 12 metre high base. In the centre, inside a great pillar, there was a small square area that must have been Augustus' tomb. A significant fact is that this area corresponded perfectly to the bronze statue of the emperor on top of the monument.

The tombs of the emperor's family are in the three most external radial walls. Here lay Marcellus, Agrippa, Drusus, Gaius and Lucius Caesar (all designated heirs by Augustus but they died prematurely), then Livia and Tiberius.

Nero was excluded from the family tomb, as Augustus' daughter Julia had been on account of her immoral behaviour. In front of the entrance to the Mausoleum there were two obelisks and, fixed to two pillars, the bronze plates bearing the *Res Gestae*, Augustus' autobiography.

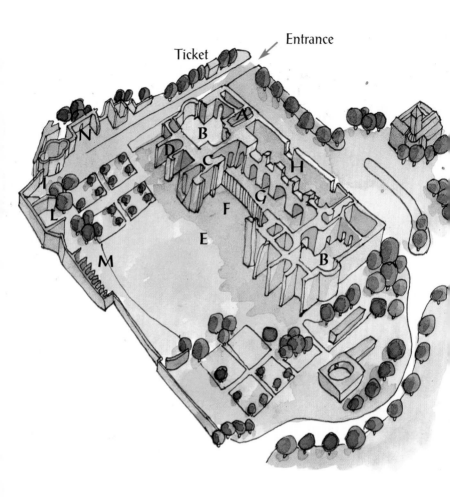

A. Apodyterium (changing room)
B. Gyms
C. Destricarium
D. *Laconicun (sauna)*
E. *Calidarium*
F. Tepidarium
G. Frigidorium
H. Natatio (pool)
I. Grand staircase
L. Libraries
M. Tanks
N. Exedra

THE BATHS OF CARACALLA

Viale delle Terme di Caracalla 52
Tel. 06.5740796

Tues.- Sat.: 9.00 -16.00. (leave by 17.00)
Sunday and Holidays: 9.00 - 12.00 (leave by 17.00)
Monday: 9.00 - 13.00 (leave by 14.00)
Closed: 1st May, 25th Dec., 1st Jan.

The archaeological area of the Baths of Caracalla is in open air

Estimated time: 2 hours

BATHS

The citizens of Rome had made use of "public baths" since the republican age (2nd century BC). These were places where everyone could have a hot bath without spending too much. In the beginning they were small buildings, but as they enjoyed a great success, in time bigger and bigger ones were built, equipped with all sorts of facilities: there were saunas, swimming pools at different temperatures and open spaces for gymnastics and games. The biggest baths also had libraries and refreshment kiosks.

The first big baths in Rome were built by Agrippa at the end of the 1st century BC, followed by those of Nero, Titus, Trajan, Caracalla, Diocletian and Constantine, to name only a few of the "imperial baths". But lots of these buildings sprung up all over the city. Just think that at the end of the imperial age there were almost 1000 of them! The baths were open from morning till sunset and were used by people of all ages and all social classes.

Being open to everybody, including layabouts, and very crowded, theft and confidence tricks were common and gambling often went on.
There was even a name for thieves who operated in the baths: *fures balneari*. Punishment was severe and ran from forced labour to exile.

Cures at the baths were advised by doctors and usually based on the healthy change from hot to cold and back to hot again.

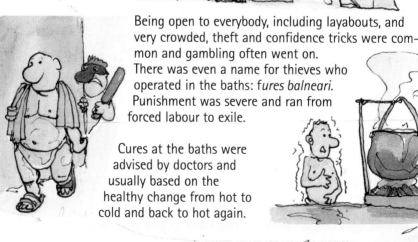

BATHS OF CARACALLA

Before going in look at the grandiose walls that enclosed the baths: they form a huge square of 12.000 square metres. The building could hold 1600 people!

The best way to visit the baths is to imagine that you're a Roman citizen about to spend a pleasant day here.
Follow the map carefully and look for the letters corresponding to the places described.
And don't forget that from now on you're a Roman citizen of the 3rd century AD!

Today you've decided on the Baths of Caracalla, built at the beginning of the 3rd century AD by the emperor Septimius Severus and completed by his son Caracalla.

Septimius Severus   *Caracalla*

Of course you'll be well kitted out! You'll have large towels, linen and woollen hand-towels, some soda (there wasn't any soap then) and maybe a pair of clogs.

If you're the athletic type and like gymnastics you'll have brought a few little containers of oils and creams to cover your body with before going into the gym, and of course a strigil, a metal blade used for getting the oil off your body after the gym, an operation made easier by the use of fine sand which you'll find available for exactly this purpose.

At this point go into the archaeological area and follow the path. On the left you'll see the big central structure of the baths. To get in you have to walk down to the end of it and, immediately to the left, go through the arched door-way. This entrance doesn't correspond to the ancient one.

First of all you ought to know that this structure, at opposite sides of the central part, is a duplication of the same area: changing rooms, gyms and saunas that are also identically decorated as you can see from the remains of the mosaics. Start from one side and make your way to the opposite one which you will see is almost identical.

The first thing to do is to find the changing room (in Latin apody-terium) shown at point (A) on the map. To be quite sure you get the right room, look for a floor like the one in the photo.

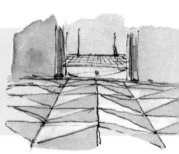

It was an unheated room with marble or brickwork benches along the walls where you could sit down on comfortable cushions and get changed. It was furnished with carpets, curtains and reclining chairs. You can leave your clothes in one of the niches (you can't see them

now, but they were like modern cupboards). For a small tip an attendant will keep an eye out for thieves. If you've left your cloak at home you'd better borrow one, you'll need it after your workout in the gym. Note the beautiful mosaic floor. We wouldn't use such a luxurious type of decoration now but in those days material and labour cost much less. So baths were almost always decorated with splendid mosaics in precious tesserae depicting scenes linked to the world of water and the sea: waves, fish, dolphins, nymphs and tritons.

Now you're ready for the gym. Go back to the first big room you went into (B), passing through a high covered area and turning right.

You're in an open space. Here you can do running, gymnastics, wrestling, boxing, fencing or the all-time favourite Roman sport, play ball. The rhyme goes: *"At Caracalla's Baths they say, ball the Romans used to play"*.

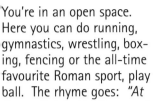

The three areas at the bottom are for indoor exercises, for oiling yourself in preparation for the gym or for enjoying a bracing massage to relax your muscles after all the effort. If you're a girl you might prefer to play with a hoop or ball, or train with various kinds of weights. If you're a very energetic sort of person you can also do a bit of wrestling. But it isn't considered very elegant!

Let your imagination take over: these high walls were covered with precious marble and decorated with thousand-coloured paintings and stucco-work. Along the sides there was a porticoed area with columns and with a terrace above it.

Now you're tired and you want a sauna.

Leave the gym and look for areas marked (C). Today they are closed off by a gate.

They were called *destrictaria* and were heated. There are servants here who will wash you down and rub your body until you're ready for the sauna. The saunas known as *sudatoria* (D) are beyond these rooms.

If you want to see them you have to go all the way round and look from outside.

After the sweat bath has purified your body and relaxed your tired muscles you go to the caldarium or calidarium (E).

It was a great round room with a large, glazed arch-window to receive the light and heat of the sun throughout the day. There was a big, round hot water pool in the middle.

You go down the steps and plunge in for a completely relaxing bath.

But you don't stay there too long: to tone up your muscles you have to move on gradually to cooler temperatures.

So on you go to the tepidarium (F), a small room where you can have a lukewarm bath. You can get a glimpse of it behind a black gate on the same side of the destrictarium, a bit farther on.

Now it's time for the freezing cold bath. Hard line believers in the tradition of the tough, austere Roman will have skipped the hot baths and come straight here.
Check your position on the map and look around. You're already in the gigantic rectangular room called the *frigidarium* (G), the centre of the complex.

There are several pools full of cold water.

You can see them at the sides of the room with their steps for getting in.

In ancient times there were also two great marble baths in two side rooms. Now they are in Piazza Farnese.

As well as these small pools the Baths also have a big swimming pool (H) where you can really get moving: go back, turn right as if you were going to the changing rooms and you'll see it on the right. You can go down the steps and dive in. When you're tired go back to the changing rooms and get dressed.

Before leaving the central area of the Baths, try this game. But watch out! Remember everything you've seen up to now, check the map for the names of the various rooms and, most of all, remember that

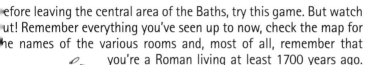

you're a Roman living at least 1700 years ago. Ready?

Time yourself to see how long you take to finish.

1. You want to say hello to a friend who usually uses the **changing room** opposite yours.
Keeping in mind that they are symmetrical and have the same kind of floor, go and look for him. Got it? (Check the photo of the floor you saw at the beginning).

2. Somebody tells you they saw him near this column. Find the column.

3. When you arrive your friend isn't there any more. But looking around you seem to spot him in the crowded *frigidarium*. He's walking by the right hand wall towards the *natatio*.

4. There are a lot of mosaic fragments there now, including this one. Found it? But unfortunately your friend isn't there. You mistook somebody else for him: everybody's dressed in white and more or less in the same way.

5. You ask an acquaintance who tells you that your friend is taking a cold bath in one of the pools at the opposite side of the *frigidarium*. Look for it carefully, it's the only one of this shape. Go there.

There he is! You recognize him from behind and you go up and splash him. Oh no, you've done it again! You've just splashed his brother! Your friend has gone to look for you in your changing room, but

anyway he'll be waiting for you at the usual plac

WHERE'S THE USUAL PLACE?

6. To find out you have to go back towards your own changing roon going into the covered area, after which you'll see the *natatio* on th right and the changing room on the left. And there's your frien leaning against the wall on the right.

He's one of the three i the drawing. If you got t the right place, a certai detail will tell you whic one is him and you'll b the winner! Otherwis start again! (But chec the solution anyway).
If you took less tha twenty minutes, you'v proved that you're a reg ular here at the Bath. Congratulations!

Now go out of the central area of the Baths and, if you aren't too tired, before going back follow this itinerary again which will take you to the external enclosure where there are some grandiose ruin. of the buildings that once stood nearby. Once again take the path that runs from the ticket office and follow it to the end where it turn. the corner to the left.

Right there at the corner of the path you can see, if you look carefully, what is left of the grand staircase (I). People arriving from the Aventine entered the baths here.

Immediately on the left of these steps are the remains of another large place, the library (L).

There were niches along the walls for the large cupboards that contained the *volumina*.

The Romans had built a system of cavity walls which insulated them perfectly from humidity which would have damaged them beyond repair. The ruins you see on the left of the library were part of the tanks (M) where they stored the water that was carried to the various parts of the building by a complex system of canals and pipes.

Going back towards the ticket office, once you've passed the library and the staircase you'll find you're walking alongside a high semi-circular wall.

These are the remains of the great exedra (N) of the enclosure (there's an identical one on the opposite side). There were three large communicating rooms here for festivals and banquets. These gatherings were organised in a very sophisticated way: archaeologists have even found the remains of a complex system for spreading perfume around.

Imagine you're a rich Roman and you've been invited to dinner at the baths. You won't just enjoy refined dishes, dancing and music: the air will seem especially heady because of the essences gradually released into the air.

HISTORY AND
LEGENDS

THE FOUNDING OF ROME

Nobody knows the true history of the founding of Rome.
The Romans invented fine legends to explain how their city was founded, and they chose 21st April 753 BC as the day of its founding. The legends about the birth of Rome have become so famous that it's worthwhile telling a few of them.

The Landing of Aeneas
Aeneas was an inhabitant of Troy in Asia Minor (today Turkey). During the siege of his city he managed to escape with his son Ascanius and, after a thousand adventures, landed on the coast of Latium near the mouth of the Tiber.
After many years Numitor became king of Alba Longa (a city in Latium founded by Aeneas' son) but his brother Amulius decided to depose him and seize the throne. Numitor had a daughter, Rea Silvia, whom Amulius forced to become a priestess of Vesta so that she would not be able to have children. The legend says that Rea Silvia was so beautiful that the god Mars fell in love with her and they had twins together. Amulius was not at all pleased with this so he took the twins and abandoned them to the river Tiber in a basket.

ROMULUS AND REMUS

All abandoned in a basket
on a Tiber river bank,
the poor Twins raised a racket
as their bellies rather shrank.

A she-wolf went by that spot
and took pity on the poor cubs:
fresh milk they needed a lot
and some good tail back-rubs.

So she adopted them with all speed
and she hugged them to her heart.
The Twins wolfed down their feed
and grew up strong and smart.

When the wolf was out shopping,
an old shepherd found the two boys
in their basket quietly sleeping
among bones that were their toys.

So he took them to his good lady
who happened to know their real mother.
To welcome them back she was ready
because she had missed them, rather.

She had to explain the whole story
and it took her quite a bit.
At the end the Twins felt bound for glory
and decided to go look for it.

e best way to earn one's glory
to go to the nearest town, but tere's the pity,
ere was none around their territory:
they thought to build their own city.

e only flaw in this great vision
that two kings is a king too much:
ey had to take a hard decision
d they chose a bird-watching
atch.

After counting six fat sparrows
mus came down to claim his crown
t Romulus shook at him his arrows:
welve blackbirds: hand it down!"

He plowed a circle and laid a plan,
built the first house and called it home,
kicked out his brother on a ban:
he elected himself first king of Rome.

THE RAPE OF THE SABINE WOMEN

In order to populate Rome in a short period Romulus opened an "asylum" where fugitives from nearby cities could find refuge. Rome immediately filled up, but mainly with men, so Romulus thought up a scheme to get wives for them.

*All we need to begin our lives
is to pull a trick so smart
as to get us some nice wives
so our families we can start.*

*The only one who's got the brain
to solve this puzzle it's me, your king.
You do not need your mind to strain;
this is how our life will swing.*

*The Sabines, we all know, are so cautious,
guard their women like precious pearls,
but I bet we can cheat Titus Tatius
and his subjects of all their girls.*

*We'll invite them for wine and dancing:
then, when the party is at its peak
and the drunks begin to sing,
listen hard to my whistle squeak:*

*That's the signal to grab your partner
and start running for dear life.
If you're fast and do not hurt her
each of you will have a wife!"*

*So they did and were so quick
that old King Tatius ranted and swore:
"Of all our girls you took your pick.
Where's my army? To War! To War!"*

TARPEIA

The Sabines could not succeed in breaching the walls of Rome by force of arms so their king Titus Tatius convinced Tarpeia, daughter of the commander of the Capitol, to help them enter the city.

In exchange Tarpeia was to receive a gift of what the Sabines wore on their left arm (bracelets and jewels, Tarpeia thought). When the Sabines entered Rome they gave Tarpeia what they actually wore on their left arm - their shields - and she died under the weight of the heavy armour.

So the Sabines entered Rome.

They went straight through the gate
ready to bite like dogs gone wild...
but the Sabines had to stop and wait:
the first thing they saw was a child

who looked a lot like someone they knew!
Many more babies were crawling around
and they all looked very familiar, too!
Daughters and sisters happy they found

with their Roman husbands holding hands.
See old King Tatius: now he looks so mild,
he's dropped his weapons and there he stands
hugging his daughter and his grandchild!

One cannot with in-laws well fight,
so they shook hands and forgot
the past.
One big family is a beautiful sight
and the new town filled up fast.

Tradition tells us that there were seven kings of Rome. Romulus, Numa Pompilius, Tullus Hostilius, Ancus Marcius, Tarquinius Priscus, Servius Tullius and Tarquin the Proud. When the last king was got rid of (Tarquin the Proud) Rome was declared a Republic.

THE CAPITOLINE GEESE

Rome suffered one of its worst defeats in 390 BC near the river Allia at the hands of Brennus, leader of the Gauls.

A lot of the inhabitants fled, some hid on the Capitoline hill, and the senators waited motionless in the Senate for the arrival of the enemy in Rome. When the fairly barbarian Gauls found the senators all motionless they thought they weren't real. As a test a Gaul pulled a senator's beard. The senator was furious and started slapping the invader. The senators were all killed. Brennus sacked Rome and then tried by cunning to breach the Capitoline Hill where a lot of the city's treasures were hidden. He attacked by night, counting on the element of surprise.

On Capitol Hill, through the night,
Romans for once forgot their war:
they would rather sleep tight,
have sweet dreams and perhaps snore.

Only the Gauls were wide awake
and ready to climb up to the top.
They were sneaky more than a snake
and nobody could tell them to stop.

That's no way to fight a battle:
one army quietly climbs up the hill
while the other snores like a rattle,
peacefully dreaming, an easy kill.

There was only a fat Roman goose
that on Capitol Hill could not sleep:
she saw the Gauls and hell broke loose,
so loud she squawked they had to leap.

Quawk-quawk!" cried the geese,
"Quawk-quawk!" cried the ganders,
and only went back to sleep in peace
when told so by their commanders.

After 7 whole months of siege Brennus still hadn't managed to breach the Capitol, so he decided that he would pack up and go home if the Romans gave him 1.000 gold liras.

But the scales were fixed and the Romans complained of the trick. Brennus shouted "Vae victis" (which means "Woe to the defeated") and threw his sword onto the scales in order to obtain even more gold. At this point Camillus, a valiant Roman, shouted, "Not with gold but with iron do we defend the motherland," unsheathed his sword and began a furious fight against the Gauls, in the end succeeding in making them flee.

We cannot say with certainty whether these deeds are historically accurate or not, but we know that the Romans had a great fear of the Gauls until Julius Caesar had conquered and subjugated the whole of Gaul.

JULIUS CAESAR

Gaius Julius Caesar is one of the greatest men in known history. Gaius was his first name, Julius his father's name in accordance with Roman custom, and Caesar his *cog nomen* or surname.

He was a man of many qualities: intelligent, courageous and generous, a brave general, a skilled politician and an important writer. He wasn't handsome, always worrying about his baldness and trying everything to hide it, but women liked him immensely.

He was born in Rome around 101 BC of a noble but not wealthy family. Like all Roman boys of good family he studied Greek and Latin. His teacher, Gripho, was a native of Gaul, a land which Caesar would conquer and subjugate years later.

Caesar boasted of being a descendant of Julius, son of Aeneas and grandson of the goddess Venus, and of Ancus Martius, one of Rome's seven kings. We don't know if that's true, but he certainly did have an important uncle: Marius, the great general who led the rebellion of the people against the senatorial aristocracy.

In that period Rome had been thrown into confusion by power struggles. The aristocracy of the senate governed with difficulty: wealth and property were in the hands of a small group of landowners, and the people, who lived in a state of great poverty, tended to rebel. Caesar followed his uncle Marius' example, but he went a lot farther.

In politics Caesar always tried to win the people's sympathy but he was also very good at forming alliances with the most powerful men in Rome. He made an agreement with Crassus, who was extremely rich, and Pompey, the leader of the senatorial aristocracy. This was the First Triumvirate (*tres viri* means three men).

In war Caesar was a bold commander, always in the front line, and above all a strategic genius.
His most important exploit was the conquest of Gaul. His book *De Bello Gallico* is a well written and fascinating account of the campaign.

HISTORY AND LEGENDS

When Caesar became very powerful, adored by his faithful army, loved by the people and rich from the spoils of war, his precarious relationship with Pompey and the senate turned into open conflict.

That's how the Rubicon, a little river that separated Rome from Cisalpine Gaul, became famous all over the world. There was a law forbidding generals to cross this river with their armies and approach the capital under arms. On his way back from Gaul Caesar had to make a crucial decision: either respect the law or march on Rome against the senate and Pompey. When he was sure about what he wanted to do he said: "*Alea iacta est!*" (the die is cast), crossed the Rubicon and marched on Rome.

Pompey and many of the senators fled. Caesar followed them to Spain and Africa and defeated them.

In Egypt he got to know the fascinating Cleopatra. Though already married to his fourth wife, Calpurnia, he allowed the queen of Egypt to seduce him and took a long holiday with her on the Nile. When he came home and was elected dictator for life, Rome was his. He was lenient with those who had fought against him, but that wasn't enough. In republican Rome a man who held all the power, even if the crown he chose to wear was only a laurel wreath, seemed too much like a king!

On the morning of 15th March 44 BC Caesar was killed, stabbed 23 times by a group of senators in the Theatre of Pompey. In his hand he held a scroll in which someone had warned him of the plot but he didn't read it in time. Caesar fell, right at the foot of the statue of his old rival Pompey. One of the assassins was his adopted son Brutus, to whom Caesar is said to have addressed the famous words: "*Tu quoque Brute, fili mi!*" (you too Brutus, my son!)

GAIUS JULIUS CAESAR OCTAVIANUS AUGUSTUS

This long name stands for different phases in the life of the emperor Augustus.

Gaius Octavius wasn't a very strong child, he was often ill and was very studious. He didn't seem very suitable for military life and nobody thought he would go very far.

He was 19 when he heard that his grandmother's bro-ther, Julius Caesar, had been murdered and that he, Gaius Octavius, was his heir.

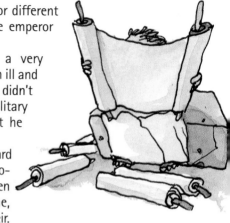

Caesar had no legitimate children. Maybe he chose Gaius Octavius because in spite of being frail he showed great will power and intelligence.

Gaius Julius Caesar Octavianus' first gesture (by now he had taken his adoptive father's name and surname) was to distribute Julius Caesar's wealth to the citizens and soldiers in accordance with Caesar's will. In this way he immediately showed that he didn't want to inherit Caesar's material possessions but rather his political greatness and prestige.

At first Octavian allied himself with the Senate against Mark Antony and defeated him at Modena. But then he decided to go against the Senate, prefer-ring to make a pact with Mark Antony and Lepidus. This was the Second Triumvirate. The three men governed for some years, fighting all the defenders of republican institutions,

including the conspirators who had assassinated Caesar. Brutus, who had a dream in which Caesar said threateningly, "We shall meet again at Philippi", in fact died at Philippi in one of these battles.

Octavian, Mark Antony and Lepidus shared out the Roman world: Lepidus got Africa, Octavian got Italy and the West, Antony the East. Lepidus later chose to abandon politics and enjoy his riches.

In Egypt Antony ended up in Cleopatra's net, fell in love and married her. He remained in the East and forgot his native country.

Augustus then convinced Rome to declare war on Mark Antony and Cleopatra who were defeated at the battle of Actium in 31 BC. Antony killed himself. Cleopatra, who tried unsuccessfully to seduce Octavian, later committed suicide by having a poisonous snake bite her.

At the age of 32 Octavian was alone in command. For decades Rome had been torn by civil wars, power struggles and conspiracies: a new system of government was needed.

Octavian took great care to exercise his immense power without irritating the Romans. He led a simple life, worked uninterruptedly for the State, appeared modest and showed respect for the republican institutions which called for consuls, senate, comitia and all the other public offices.

He invented the *consilium principis*, a group of experts in the various sectors of the State who collaborated with him. At the same time he managed to continually increase his prestige to the extent of being deified.

In 27 BC he had the title *Augustus* conferred on him, a name previously reserved for gods. He governed well for many years, successfully keeping the so-named "*pax romana*" until his death at the age of about 80 in the year 14 AD.

NERO

Even if baby looks less than zero
his mum still likes him - thus with Nero.
Agrippina day and night
intrigued so that one day she might
see her son, her very own
sitting on the Empire throne.

Seneca and Burrus were sent by mummy
To teach him not to be a dummy
but our young Nero, not the smartest,
thought himself the perfect artist.
Commanding didn't mean a thing,
he only wanted to play and sing.

Poppea Sabina he got to meet
(Far more cruel than she was sweet)
and this is why they say "that woman
turned Nero into a raving demon:
to please his little wife Sabina, he
murdered his mother Agrippina".

See him as he spends and spends
governing without good sense,
poetry's what he loves so well
under Petronius' cultured spell.
And partying both day and night
He lost his head, as well he might.

He thought he was a star of fame
but mad and bad Nero became,
and that is why when Rome burnt dow
a lot of people in the town
said "All his fault, this great disaster
is all the fault of our crazy master".

TRAJAN, OPTIMUS PRINCEPS

When Trajan was proclaimed emperor on the death of Nerva (98 AD) he was 45 years old and fighting to defend the frontiers of the Empire on the River Rhine. He let it be known that he would come to Rome as soon as he could, but not immediately because he wanted to bring his war to a close.

So right from the start he showed himself to be a man of steadfast character, not the type to let power go to his head.

He was born in Italica, a Spanish city. He was the first man from the provinces to become emperor. The political classes had understood that it was time to open up to people who had not been born in Rome. Trajan in fact served the State much better than certain of his predecessors.

He made important conquests: Dacia, Armenia, Syria, Mesopotamia and Persia, extending the Empire as never before.

From 98 AD until his death in 117 AD Trajan governed wisely and prudently. He increased the spread of agriculture and was very involved in helping the poor, especially children. The historian Pliny the Younger wrote: "A grand thing, Caesar, to feed the hope of Rome at your expense."

Trajan undertook a great many public works, leaving a stupendous token of his reign: the most important include the Trajan Way, which ran from Benevento to Brindisi, the Segovia aqueduct, the Verona amphitheatre, the port of Ostia, the Forum of Trajan and the famous Column.

In 114 AD the senate awarded him the title "*Optimus Princeps*" (the best of princes). This was an expression of Rome and the empire's sincere recognition of Trajan's great value.

HADRIAN

Trajan chose Hadrian as his successor, Spaniard like himself. His statues are easily recognisable because of his fine beard! He was a very able administrator and invented an extremely efficient system for collecting taxes even from the most distant provinces of the Empire. He decided on a policy of peace and limited himself to defending the territories that Trajan had conquered. For example, he built the famous Hadrian's Wall that marked the frontier of the Empire in Great Britain and kept the barbarians out. He also left other great monuments such as Hadrian's Villa in Tivoli which you can go and see.

Hadrian, as is well known,
Followed Trajan on the throne.
A man so cultured and refined
As to nearly blow your mind.

He loved beauty most of all,
he was an artist and a poet,
but built much more than just his Wall
(in case you don't already know it).

He took no risks with great bold
deeds but kept the frontiers well
defended, governed wisely and
kept the peaceexactly as he had
intended.

Over the mountains, here and there,
seas and rivers, everywhere,
with zeal and commitment you'll admire
he rearranged his great Empire.

But sometimes he would feel quite bad,
silent and gloomy, worried, sad.
A strangely fascinating man
the great, great Emperor Hadrian:

one day he'd be all bright and jolly
the next he'd be all melancholy.
A veil of sadness seemed to cover
something in this beauty-lover.

CARACALLA

With Septimius Severus dead
the Empire went to his sons instead
but Caracalla's worst was shown
as soon as he got to the throne.

He didn't want to share, no fear!
so made his brother disappear:
he killed poor Geta one fine day
just to get his own spoilt way.

Felines were his favourite fun,
lions and tigers: he slept with one
and with the other breakfast took,
just kittens in Caracalla's book.

Though very good with his savage cat,
as a general he fell quite flat:
maybe that's why so many were filled
with hate for him and had him killed.

Caracalla is famous for
the Edict but not a whole lot more:
the Baths and then the fact that he
governed the Empire heartlessly.

Caracalla governed from 211 to 217
AD. With the famous Edict of 212 he extended Roman citizenship to all
inhabitants of the provinces, the final step in putting the provinces on an
equal level with Rome.

The history of the Roman Empire doesn't end with Caracalla. There were
periods of unrest and anarchy alternated with the reigns of great emperors like Diocletian and Constantine.
The difficult internal and external problems - the government of Rome
and its immense possessions and the defence of the frontiers against
barbarian invasions - led to the division of the Empire into Western
Empire and Eastern Empire and finally to the fall of the Western Roman
Empire in 476 AD. The spread of Christianity and the choice of Rome as
the Pope's residence bore witness to an ancient and vast empire and gave
the city a new central function.
With its rich history Rome would remain the Eternal City for people of all
periods.

USEFUL INFORMATION

For information about the main museums, monuments, exhibition and services in Rome, including temporary events for children and young people, contact:

Azienda di Promozione Turistica of Rome
via Parigi, 5 tel. 06.488.99255

The Postazioni Informative of the Commune of Rome
(open 9 a.m. 6 p.m.)

Largo Goldoni (via del Corso)   Tel. 06.68136061

Piazza San Giovanni in Laterano   Tel. 06.77203535

Via Nazionale (in front of Palazzo delle Esposizioni) Tel. 06.4782452

Piazza delle Cinque Lune   Tel. 06.68809240

Lungotevere Castel Sant'Angelo (piazza Pia)   Tel. 06.6880970

Piazza del Tempio della Pace (Fori Imperiali)   Tel. 06.699243C

Piazza Sonnino (Trastevere)   Tel. 06.5833345

Santa Maria Maggiore (via dell'Olmata)   Tel. 06.4740955

Piazza dei Cinquecento (Termini)   Tel. 06.4782519

Stazione Termini   Tel. 06.4890630

Via Minghetti   Tel. 06.6782988

Internet page for on-line information:
HYPERLINK http://www.comune.roma.it www.comune.roma.it
Various information, including a children's section.
www.informaroma.it
or
Commune Information **on page 601 Televideo Rai 3**

SOLUTIONS TO GAMES

. 16 The internal space of the Basilica Emilia was divided into 4 naves.

. 18 In Roman times, cell phones, glasses, ball point pens and watches did not exist.

. 20 The exact order of the triumph scones is: E, B, D, A, C.

. 24 The child dressed in purple does not go in.

. 30 The Vestal who does not have a pedastal is n° 6. The others have respectively: 1-B, 2-A, 3-E, 4-C, 5-D.

. 33 If you have followed the route suggested by this guide you will already have seen the Temple of Divus Iulius that was dedicated to Julius Caesar after his death.

. 36 The Arch of Titus has 1 arch, while that of Septimius Severus has 3.

. 57 The exact answers are [1] C, [2] C, [3] A, [4] B.

. 59 Looking at the 8 statues of the Daci you should have discovered that: 1) The statue rebuilt in '700 is that on the south side (towards Via di San Gregorio); you will recognize it because it is built entirely of white marble.
2) Not all the Daci wear a cap.
3) They all have their hands crossed but not in the same way.

. 62 Solution to the questions: *(portico capitals)* 12- *(columns)* 3 + *(stab wounds that killed Caesar)* 23 = 32.

. 65 The Palatine hill is not shown in the picture.

. 66 The strange ladder suspended in the air is because it belonged to a building which no longer exists, and it was built when the ground level was much higher than today.

. 104 The exact phrase is: Many emperor's constructed buildings to win the love of the people.

. 112 The exact answers are: [1] B/C in fact the obelisk that he is holding is the hand of a sun dial; [2] B; [3] C.

. 124 Your friend is second in line, dressed in yellow under the painting with the Madonnina).